PREFACE

I remember the first time I was promoted to a leadership position. The excitement was undeniable—a recognition of my hard work and expertise. But along with the thrill came a series of questions and, if I'm honest, a fair amount of self-doubt. Suddenly, the skills that had brought me this far didn't seem as useful in a role where my success depended on the success of others. Like so many new leaders, I quickly realized that stepping into this role wasn't simply about applying my previous skills on a larger scale; it was about building an entirely new set of skills, a new mindset, and a new sense of responsibility.

The journey from rookie to leader is an adventure filled with learning curves, challenges, and rewarding moments. It's a path I navigated with mixed success early on, often fumbling through trial and error. With time, I realized that the most valuable lessons didn't come from having all the answers but from embracing the process of growth, self-discovery, and the humility that comes with knowing I didn't have to be perfect. What I needed was a willingness to learn, adapt, and continually improve—for my team, for the organization, and myself.

This book is my attempt to offer you a roadmap that I wish I ha It's a guide to help you navigate the complexities of your new role w insight, clarity, and confidence. Whether you're stepping intc leadership position for the first time or looking to refresh y approach, I hope this book will serve as both a companion a mentor, equipping you with the tools you need to face the chall ahead.

I've written this book because I believe that great leadersh reserved for the naturally gifted or those with years of experienc leadership emerges from a commitment to growth, an oper learning from both successes and mistakes and a genuine make a positive impact on others. Becoming a leader is about not perfection. The goal isn't to become flawless but to someone others trust, respect, and willingly follow.

So, if you're here, standing on the edge of this new ch that you're not alone. The challenges and uncertainties are are the rewards of growing into a leader who makes a diffe this book helps you find confidence in your unique reminds you that the path to great leadership is a journ taking.

Thank you for letting me be a part of it.

Contents

From Rookie To Leader

Mastering The Art Of Effective Leadership

Jerry Brittain

.

INTRODUCTION

Stepping into a leadership role for the first time is a profound moment in your life. It's thrilling, a little daunting, and completely transformative. It's not just about doing more—it's about becoming more. Suddenly, you're not just accountable for your work; you're entrusted with the success, growth, and well-being of an entire team. That shift can feel overwhelming, but it's also an incredible opportunity to discover who you are and what kind of impact you're capable of making.

If you're here, it's because you're ready to take that step. You're ready to lead. And that's what this book is about—helping you navigate this exciting, sometimes messy, always rewarding journey.

"From Rookie to Leader" was written with new leaders in mind—those stepping into uncharted territory for the first time. It's a guide, a toolkit, and, hopefully, a source of encouragement as you learn what it takes to inspire others and create meaningful results. Leadership isn't about having all the answers or being perfect. It's about growth—yours and the people you lead. It's about showing up every day with humility, curiosity, and a willingness to learn.

This book will help you tackle some of the most common challenges you'll face as a new leader—building trust, having tough conversations, and making decisions that matter. But it's not just about strategies or checklists. True leadership starts within. We'll explore what it means to understand yourself, articulate your values, and align your actions with a purpose bigger than yourself. When you lead authentically and clearly, people follow—not because they have to, but because they want to.

Let's be honest: stepping into leadership can feel a little like being thrown into the deep end of the pool. There will be moments when you're not sure you're ready, moments when doubt creeps in. That's okay. The best leaders aren't the ones who pretend they have it all figured out—they're the ones who embrace the learning process, who listen, adapt, and grow.

Leadership isn't a box you check or a title you earn. It's a practice. A journey. One that evolves with every challenge, every conversation, and every step forward. The goal isn't perfection—it's progress. It's becoming the kind of leader people trust, respect, and want to follow because they see how much you care.

So, welcome. This is where your journey begins. You have the opportunity to create something significant, not just for yourself but for the people you lead. Together, we'll explore how to turn that opportunity into a reality.

Let's get started.

Entering the leadership mindset

The Shift from Individual Contributor to Leader

Stepping into a leadership role is a profound moment of transformation. It's exhilarating—finally, you have the chance to make an impact on a bigger stage. But let's be honest: it's also a little daunting. You're not just adding a new title to your résumé; you're stepping into a role that will challenge you in ways you never anticipated. This transition marks a shift, not just in what you do, but in how you think, how you measure success, and how you inspire others.

At its core, the move from individual contributor to leader is about expanding your focus—from the success of one (you) to the success of many (your team). It's no longer just about what you accomplish. Now, your true impact lies in your ability to create an environment where others can thrive, grow, and achieve great things. The spotlight shifts from you to your team—and that's where the magic of leadership begins.

One of the most fundamental changes you'll encounter as a leader is this: it's no longer about you. It's about us. This shift from "I" to "we" might seem simple on the surface, but it can feel surprisingly uncomfortable at first. After all, up until now, your success has been yours to own—your hard work, your skills, your results. As a leader, though, your success is measured not by what you achieve, but by what your team achieves.

This isn't just a matter of semantics. It's a profound shift in mindset. Your job is no longer to be the star performer; it's to help others shine. Leadership isn't about standing out—it's about standing behind, beside, and sometimes even in front of your team, depending on what they need in the moment. When your team wins, you win. When they struggle, it's not a failure—it's an opportunity for you to guide, support, and help them grow.

Think of it this way: in your previous role, the work you put in often led directly to personal recognition. A job well done came with a pat on the back, a bonus, or maybe even a promotion. But now, your role is to help your team achieve that recognition. Your satisfaction will come not from what you accomplish individually but from seeing your team succeed. Their wins are your wins. Their growth is your legacy.

To embrace this shift, start by celebrating collective achievements. If your team hits a milestone, resist the urge to take credit—even if you played a significant role. Instead, focus on shining the light on them. When challenges arise, approach them as shared obstacles, not individual failures. The more you lean into "we," the more you'll create a sense of unity and purpose within your team. And when people feel like they're part of something bigger than themselves, amazing things happen.

In your previous role, solving problems yourself was often a badge of honor—a sign of reliability, competence, and hard work. But as a leader, your strength is no longer defined by what you can do alone. Leadership is about empowering others to solve problems, make decisions, and take ownership of their work. It's about building capacity within your team, helping each person grow into their potential.

Think of leadership as gardening. Your job isn't to grow the plants yourself but to create the conditions where they can thrive—providing sunlight, water, and nutrients. Similarly, your team needs guidance, encouragement, and the right opportunities to flourish. This doesn't mean stepping back and letting go entirely; it means stepping forward with intentionality. When a challenge arises, resist the urge to swoop in with a solution. Instead, try asking, What do you think we should do? or How would you approach this? Lead with questions that spark their thinking and show your belief in their abilities.

Empowering others isn't just about delegation—it's about trust. It's about believing that your team is capable and then giving them the room to prove it. Yes, it might feel uncomfortable at first. Letting go of control always does. But every time you give your team the chance to step up, you're not just solving today's problem; you're building their confidence and capabilities for tomorrow. And that is what leadership is all about.

One of the biggest shifts you'll face as a leader is how you measure success. In your previous role, success was likely tied to your personal output—how fast, how accurate, how innovative you could be. But leadership rewrites the rules. Your success is no longer just about you; it's about them. It's about how your team performs, how they grow, and how they come together to achieve something greater than any one person could accomplish alone.

Think of your team as an ecosystem. When every individual is healthy, supported, and thriving, the entire system flourishes. But when one part of the system struggles, it creates ripples that affect everyone. Your role as a leader is to nurture that ecosystem—to identify when someone is struggling and help them overcome it, and to celebrate when someone excels, knowing that their success reflects the strength of the environment you've built.

The metrics change too. Employee satisfaction, engagement,

retention, and team cohesion—these are the benchmarks of effective leadership. Success becomes less about the short-term wins and more about creating a culture of sustained excellence. A culture where people feel valued, supported, and motivated to do their best work. When your team wins, you win. When they grow, you grow.

As a leader, the legacy you leave isn't measured in personal accolades or individual contributions. It's measured in the impact you've had on others—their growth, their success, and the inspiration they carry forward because of your influence. That's the real mark of leadership.

One of the hardest lessons for new leaders to learn is that perfection is not the goal. In your previous role, you probably prided yourself on getting the details just right, ensuring every outcome reflected your hard work and high standards. But as a leader, you'll quickly realize that striving for perfection in every task—especially through your own lens—can hold your team back. Leadership requires you to loosen your grip and trust others to take the reins, even if their methods or outcomes look different from what you might have done.

Here's the truth: perfectionism can be the enemy of progress. When you insist on things being done "your way," you risk stifling the growth and creativity of your team. Instead of perfection, focus on cultivating excellence through empowerment. Give your team the freedom to experiment, innovate, and solve problems in their own unique ways. You'll be amazed at what people can achieve when they're trusted to take ownership and think outside the box.

Letting go of perfection doesn't mean lowering your standards. It means redefining them. Success is no longer about doing everything right—it's about fostering an environment where your team feels confident to take risks, learn from mistakes, and grow. When you shift from perfectionism to trust, you not only lighten your own load but also build a culture where people feel valued and inspired to bring their best to the table.

Your team isn't just watching what you say—they're watching who you are. From day one, your actions, attitude, and values will shape the culture of your team. As a leader, you have the opportunity—and the responsibility—to set the tone for how your team operates. If you lead with integrity, openness, and respect, those qualities will ripple outward, creating a foundation for collaboration and trust.

Start by prioritizing relationships. Take the time to genuinely connect with each member of your team. Ask questions that go beyond their job titles: What drives you? What challenges are you facing? What do you want to accomplish? The more you understand your team's strengths, motivations, and aspirations, the better equipped you'll be to support them. And just as important, those conversations show your team that you care—not just about what they can do for you, but about who they are as people.

These relationships are the bedrock of effective leadership. They build trust, foster respect, and create a sense of belonging. When people feel seen and valued, they'll go above and beyond—not because they have to, but because they want to.

Leadership isn't about commanding from the top; it's about walking alongside your team, modeling the values you want to see and creating a culture where everyone feels empowered to contribute. When you prioritize people first, everything else—results, innovation, and growth—falls into place.

The Leader's Identity

Stepping into a leadership role for the first time can feel like standing at a crossroads. Who am I as a leader? What do I bring to this role? These questions are not just natural—they're necessary. Leadership isn't simply a title or a set of tasks; it's an extension of who you are. It requires clarity about your values, your strengths, and your unique perspective. Your leadership identity is the compass that guides your decisions, shapes how your team perceives you, and defines the influence you'll have.

Think of your leadership identity as your foundation. It's the core of what makes you, you, but now expressed through the lens of service to others. When you understand and embrace this identity, it becomes easier to navigate challenges, connect with your team, and lead with confidence and authenticity.

Authentic leadership begins with introspection. Take a moment to ask yourself: What are my core values? What principles do I hold dear? Maybe it's transparency, fairness, innovation, or accountability. These values aren't just personal—they are the building blocks of your leadership identity. When you lead in alignment with your values, you create a sense of authenticity that resonates with your team. People trust leaders who are consistent and true to their principles.

But here's the challenge: what happens when your personal values clash with the organizational culture? For example, you might value flexibility, yet find yourself in a rigid, results-driven environment. Moments like these can feel like an internal tug-of-war. The key isn't to abandon your values but to adapt thoughtfully. Ask yourself, How can I stay true to what matters to me while aligning with the organization's goals?

Maybe it means introducing small changes, like giving your team more autonomy within existing structures. Or perhaps it's about showing innovation in how you meet objectives, balancing the organization's priorities with your own principles. Leadership isn't about conformity—it's about creating harmony between who you are and what the organization needs.

When your leadership reflects your authentic self, you not only feel more confident—you also inspire confidence in others. People want to follow leaders who are grounded, genuine, and consistent. And when your values shine through your actions, you set a powerful example of what leadership can be: a balance of staying true to yourself while serving a greater purpose.

Your leadership style is as unique as your fingerprint. It's shaped by your personality, experiences, and values. There's no "one-size-fits-all" when it comes to leading a team; it's about finding the approach that feels authentic to you and works for your team. Some leaders thrive on collaboration, involving their team in decisions and fostering open dialogue. Others excel with a more directive approach, setting clear expectations and providing structured guidance. Both approaches—and everything in between—can be effective when used in the right context.

Start by asking yourself: What comes naturally to me? Are you someone who thrives in team discussions, or do you prefer setting the vision and letting others take the lead on execution? Knowing what feels authentic is key. But don't lock yourself into one style. Leadership is dynamic. Your team's needs, the organizational culture, and the challenges you face will all require you to adapt. The most effective leaders are those who balance staying true to themselves with the flexibility to respond to what the moment demands.

One of the best ways to refine your style is by learning from others. Look to leaders you admire. What do they do that resonates with you? Maybe it's their ability to connect with their team, their decisiveness in tough situations, or their emphasis on open communication. Don't try to imitate them outright. Instead, take inspiration and make it your own. For example, if you admire a leader who fosters transparency, think about how you can create that in your team—maybe through regular check-ins or by encouraging open feedback.

Your leadership style will evolve as you grow, and that's a good thing. The goal isn't to have all the answers or to lead in a specific way—it's to lead in a way that's authentic, adaptable, and impactful. When you align your style with your values and your team's needs, you create the conditions for trust, collaboration, and lasting success.

For new leaders, self-doubt can feel like a constant companion. You might wonder, Am I really cut out for this? The truth is, confidence isn't something you start with—it's something you build. It grows over time, with every challenge you face and every success, no matter how small. Leadership isn't about having all the answers on day one; it's about stepping into the role with openness, curiosity, and a commitment to grow.

Start by celebrating the small wins. Each time you navigate a tough conversation or guide a project to success, you're reinforcing your capacity to lead. These moments, though they may seem minor, are building blocks for your confidence. They show you—and your team—that you're capable of handling the challenges that come your way.

A powerful way to anchor your confidence is by creating a personal leadership philosophy. This isn't about crafting a polished statement to share with others; it's about defining the principles that guide you. Ask yourself: What do I stand for as a leader? Maybe it's collaboration, transparency, or fostering growth. When you're clear on your guiding principles, they serve as a compass, helping you stay grounded during uncertainty. If your philosophy emphasizes openness, for instance, you can lean on that value when navigating difficult decisions, ensuring your actions align with your beliefs.

Confidence grows as you consistently embody these principles. Over time, it becomes less about projecting an image and more about simply being who you are. People don't follow leaders because they're perfect—they follow leaders who are genuine, steady, and committed to learning. Confidence is the result of embracing the journey, one step at a time.

Leadership isn't about perfection—it's about being real. Teams are drawn to leaders who are authentic, open, and approachable. Authenticity means leading with sincerity, owning both your strengths and your vulnerabilities. It's okay to admit when you don't have all the answers. In fact, doing so shows that you're human and willing to learn alongside your team. This kind of openness builds trust, and trust is the foundation of any successful team.

Approachability goes hand in hand with authenticity. When your team feels they can come to you with questions, concerns, or ideas, it creates an atmosphere of collaboration and mutual respect. Being approachable doesn't mean trying to be everyone's best friend—it means being someone they can rely on. Small gestures, like truly listening during conversations or asking for their input, send a powerful message: I value your voice.

Your team doesn't need a flawless leader. They need someone who is willing to show up, stay present, and care deeply about their success. Over time, your authenticity and approachability will define your leadership identity. People will see you as more than a manager—they'll see you as a leader who is invested in their growth and who stays true to their values, even in the face of challenges.

Remember, leadership isn't about being perfect. It's about being real. And when you lead with authenticity, you don't just inspire confidence in yourself—you inspire confidence in those around you.

Self-Awareness as a Foundation

Self-awareness is one of the most powerful tools a leader can develop. As a new leader, it's your compass, guiding you through the complexities of team dynamics, decision-making, and personal growth. Self-awareness helps you understand how your actions, decisions, and even emotions ripple through your team. It's what enables you to navigate both the internal challenges of leadership—like staying calm under pressure—and the external ones, such as managing conflict or fostering trust.

More than just a skill, self-awareness is a mindset. It's about being intentional—about how you show up, how you engage, and how you create impact. When you cultivate self-awareness, you're better equipped to lead with authenticity, adaptability, and purpose.

Self-awareness is the foundation of emotional intelligence, the quality that separates great leaders from good ones. At its core, emotional intelligence begins with understanding yourself—your triggers, strengths, weaknesses, and the emotions that drive your actions. Why does this matter? Because in leadership, your emotions don't just belong to you. They're felt by everyone around you. A stressed, frustrated leader can unintentionally spread tension, while a calm, composed leader fosters stability and trust.

Leadership amplifies emotions. High-stakes decisions, team disagreements, and delivering critical feedback can all evoke strong reactions. Without self-awareness, it's easy to let those emotions dictate your actions—reacting instead of responding. But when you're self-aware, you can recognize what you're feeling, understand why, and choose how to move forward in a way that aligns with your values and supports your team.

Self-aware leaders create environments where trust thrives. They're consistent and intentional, which reassures their teams, even in moments of uncertainty. By understanding how your behaviors impact others, you can foster a culture of openness and respect. This doesn't mean suppressing your emotions or striving for perfection; it means being mindful of them, learning from them, and using them to lead with clarity and purpose.

Self-awareness isn't something you achieve overnight—it's a practice. The more you commit to reflecting on your actions and their impact, the more naturally it will guide your leadership. In the end, self-awareness isn't just about becoming a better leader; it's about becoming a better version of yourself, one who inspires growth and trust in those you lead.

Self-awareness begins with an honest look in the mirror. It's about understanding what you bring to the table—and where you might need to grow. For many new leaders, this process can feel uncomfortable. After all, it's easier to focus on what you do well than to confront the areas where you struggle. But the reality is, knowing both your strengths and your limitations is what allows you to lead with authenticity and purpose.

Start by identifying the qualities that have served you well in the past. Are you a creative thinker, an effective problem-solver, or a strong communicator? These strengths are your superpowers—your unique contributions to your role as a leader. Lean into them. But don't stop there. Take time to acknowledge the areas where you feel less confident, like delegating tasks, handling conflict, or managing uncertainty. Recognizing these limitations doesn't make you weak; it makes you self-aware. And self-awareness is the first step to growth.

One of the most effective ways to deepen this understanding is to seek feedback from trusted colleagues or mentors. Ask them, What do you see as my strengths? What's one area where I could improve? Their insights might reveal blind spots or offer perspectives you hadn't considered. Remember, feedback isn't criticism—it's a gift. Leaders who actively seek feedback show humility and a commitment to improvement, setting an example that inspires their team to do the same.

The goal isn't perfection; it's progress. By identifying your strengths and limitations, you're building a foundation for growth—not just for yourself, but for the team you lead.

Emotions are an inescapable part of leadership. They drive us, connect us, and motivate us. But when left unchecked, they can also undermine our best intentions. One of the most powerful aspects of self-awareness is understanding your emotional triggers—those moments or situations that spark a strong reaction. Maybe you feel defensive when receiving critical feedback, or perhaps last-minute changes make you anxious. Recognizing these triggers isn't about avoiding challenges; it's about learning to manage your responses.

The next time you feel frustration or anxiety creeping in, take a pause. Ask yourself: What am I reacting to? Why is this bothering me? How might my reaction impact my team? This reflective pause creates space between emotion and action, allowing you to respond with intention rather than reacting impulsively.

When you understand your triggers, you take back control. Instead of being ruled by emotions, you can choose how to show up in the moment. This ability to stay composed—especially under pressure—is what earns trust and respect from your team. It shows them that no matter what challenges arise, you're someone they can count on to remain steady and clear-headed.

Great leaders aren't defined by their ability to avoid emotional reactions but by their ability to manage them constructively. When you approach challenges with awareness and composure, you create an environment of stability and trust—qualities that elevate your team and reinforce your leadership.

Self-awareness isn't something you wake up with—it's something you cultivate over time. It requires a willingness to pause, reflect, and learn from your experiences. Reflection is the bridge between who you are today and the leader you aspire to become. It allows you to take stock of your journey—celebrating the wins, examining the challenges, and identifying areas for growth.

Establishing a reflective practice can be transformative. For many leaders, journaling provides a structured way to process thoughts, emotions, and lessons from the day or week. Writing things down helps you see patterns, recognize triggers, and clarify your intentions. It's not about writing a perfect narrative—it's about creating space for self-discovery. Even five minutes at the end of the day can offer profound insights into how you lead and how you can improve.

But reflection isn't just about the past—it's also about setting the stage for the future. After a challenging conversation, for example, you might reflect on what worked, what didn't, and how you could handle similar situations more effectively. By turning those insights into specific intentions—like listening more actively or approaching with greater patience—you're creating a habit of continuous self-improvement.

Some leaders also benefit from regular "self-check-ins." At the end of each week, ask yourself questions like: What did I handle well? Where did I stumble? What's one thing I can do differently next time? These moments of introspection keep you grounded and ensure you're not just reacting to events but intentionally shaping your growth as a leader. Over time, this practice builds a deeper, more consistent sense of self-awareness.

Self-awareness isn't just about personal growth—it's the foundation for building stronger relationships with your team. When you understand your strengths, you can use them intentionally to uplift and inspire others. At the same time, acknowledging your limitations makes you relatable and approachable. Your team doesn't need a perfect leader—they need a leader who is honest, human, and willing to grow.

Being self-aware also helps you understand how your emotions and behaviors affect those around you. For instance, during high-pressure moments, stress can unintentionally translate into impatience or frustration. A self-aware leader can recognize this, take a step back, and manage their emotions in a way that sets a positive tone. This ability to self-regulate not only strengthens your leadership but also creates an environment where your team feels supported, even in challenging times.

When you lead with self-awareness, you become more attuned to your team's needs. You notice when someone is struggling, recognize when they need encouragement, and listen with empathy. This creates trust, the bedrock of any strong team. People feel valued when they know their leader understands not just what they do but who they are.

Over time, this mutual understanding fosters a cohesive, connected team environment. When your team feels seen, heard, and respected, they're more likely to bring their best selves to the table. Self-awareness doesn't just make you a better leader—it inspires your team to grow alongside you.

Imposter Syndrome: Overcoming Self-Doubt

For many new leaders, stepping into a leadership role can feel like stepping into uncharted territory. Alongside the excitement, there's often an undercurrent of self-doubt. Questions start to creep in: Am I really cut out for this? What if I don't have all the answers? Do I even deserve this role? This feeling, commonly known as "imposter syndrome," is more common than you might think—especially among high-achievers. The good news? It's not a sign of failure or inadequacy. It's a sign that you care deeply about doing well.

Overcoming imposter syndrome isn't about eliminating self-doubt altogether. It's about recognizing it for what it is: a natural part of growth, a signal that you're stepping outside your comfort zone, and an opportunity to build confidence in your leadership journey.

Imposter syndrome often arises from a disconnect between perception and reality. Internally, you might feel like you don't measure up—as if your qualifications or experience aren't enough for the responsibilities you've been given. Even though you've earned your role through your skills, hard work, and potential, there's this lingering fear that you're "faking it" or that others will eventually "see through" you.

Here's the truth: imposter syndrome doesn't mean you're unqualified. In fact, it often affects high-performing individuals who set incredibly high standards for themselves. It stems from a desire to excel—a quality that has likely brought you to where you are today. The problem arises when self-doubt holds you back from embracing opportunities, taking risks, or stepping into your full potential as a leader.

Recognizing imposter syndrome for what it is—a reflection of ambition rather than inadequacy—can help you reframe your thinking. Self-doubt isn't a barrier; it's a sign that you're in a season of growth. Every great leader has faced moments of uncertainty. What sets them apart is their willingness to move forward anyway.

The first step to overcoming imposter syndrome is acknowledging it. When those nagging thoughts arise, pause and remind yourself: This is normal. It doesn't define me. Reflect on why you were chosen for this role—your skills, accomplishments, and potential. Recognize that leadership is a journey, not a destination, and no one expects you to have all the answers right away.

Developing a growth mindset can also help. Instead of focusing on perfection, focus on progress. Celebrate small wins—whether it's navigating a tough conversation, solving a problem with your team, or simply showing up with courage on a challenging day. Each success, no matter how small, reinforces your ability to lead.

Lastly, lean on your support system. Seek guidance from mentors, colleagues, or peers who have walked a similar path. Their experiences can provide perspective and remind you that you're not alone. Sometimes, simply hearing someone else say, I've been there too, is enough to quiet the voice of self-doubt.

Remember, imposter syndrome isn't something to "fix." It's a sign that you're growing, stretching, and stepping into something meaningful. Leadership isn't about being perfect—it's about being present, learning as you go, and inspiring others to do the same. Trust yourself. You're exactly where you need to be.

One of the most powerful antidotes to imposter syndrome is adopting a growth mindset—the belief that abilities and skills can be developed through effort, learning, and persistence. A growth mindset reframes challenges and moments of self-doubt as opportunities to improve, rather than signs of inadequacy. Leadership, seen through this lens, becomes a journey of continuous learning rather than a destination where you're expected to have everything figured out from the start.

When you encounter a situation that stirs up self-doubt, remind yourself: This is part of the process. Even the most seasoned leaders face challenges, make mistakes, and experience moments of uncertainty. What sets great leaders apart is their ability to see these moments as stepping stones, not roadblocks. A growth mindset encourages you to view mistakes as valuable lessons—opportunities to grow stronger, wiser, and more capable.

This shift in perspective also builds resilience. Instead of dwelling on setbacks, you learn to bounce back with curiosity and determination, ready to tackle the next challenge. Leadership isn't about having all the answers; it's about embracing the journey of becoming better every day.

Self-doubt doesn't have to be your enemy. In fact, it can be a powerful motivator when reframed with purpose. Rather than letting it chip away at your confidence, view self-doubt as a signal—a reminder that you care deeply about doing well and that there's an opportunity to grow.

Ask yourself: What is this doubt telling me? Often, it stems from a desire to be prepared and to lead effectively. Use that desire as fuel. Channel it into constructive actions, like seeking guidance from mentors, reading about leadership strategies, or practicing the skills you want to strengthen. For example, if you feel uncertain about managing team conflicts, let that uncertainty drive you to explore conflict resolution techniques or role-play scenarios with a trusted colleague.

Taking proactive steps like these transforms self-doubt into empowerment. It shows your team—and yourself—that you're committed to growth. Leadership isn't about being perfect; it's about showing up, learning, and continuously striving to improve. When you actively address areas of uncertainty, you model what it means to lead with curiosity and resilience.

Remember, self-doubt isn't a weakness—it's a sign that you're pushing yourself into new territory. By embracing a growth mindset and turning doubt into action, you're not just overcoming challenges—you're becoming the kind of leader who inspires growth in others.

Imposter syndrome thrives in isolation, feeding on the belief that you're the only one struggling with self-doubt. But the truth is, you're not alone. Reaching out to others—mentors, peers, or trusted colleagues—can make a world of difference. When you hear stories of others navigating similar challenges, it normalizes the experience and reminds you that self-doubt is a natural part of growth. Leadership isn't about never doubting yourself—it's about moving forward anyway.

Mentorship, in particular, can be a powerful tool for overcoming imposter syndrome. A good mentor doesn't just offer advice—they provide perspective. They share their own stories of uncertainty and growth, helping you see your journey through a broader lens. Mentors can also offer constructive feedback, affirming your strengths while guiding you toward improvement. Over time, their support becomes a steady reminder that growth is a process, not a destination. Knowing someone else believes in your potential can help you believe in it too.

Don't underestimate the value of peers, either. Colleagues who are navigating leadership alongside you can provide camaraderie and shared insight. Together, you can remind one another that no one leads perfectly—and that's okay. What matters is showing up, learning, and striving to do better each day.

Imposter syndrome has a way of magnifying flaws and

minimizing achievements. To combat this, make a conscious effort to celebrate your wins—no matter how small they may seem. These victories are the building blocks of confidence. Successfully navigating a tough conversation, hitting a project deadline, or even receiving a kind word from a team member— each of these moments is proof that you're making progress.

Take time to reflect on what you've accomplished. Ask yourself: What went well? What did I learn? How have I grown? By focusing on these moments, you shift your perspective from what you lack to what you're building. Leadership is a journey of incremental growth, and every step forward matters.

Creating a habit of acknowledging progress also reinforces your sense of purpose. It reminds you that you're not just filling a role—you're making a difference. Over time, these reflections help you internalize the truth: you are capable, and you are growing into the leader you aspire to be.

Building confidence as a leader isn't about erasing self-doubt—it's about learning to navigate it. Seeking support, celebrating progress, and reframing your mindset are all steps that bring you closer to your full potential. Leadership is a process of becoming, not being. Each step forward, no matter how small, is a testament to your growth. And with each step, you're creating a foundation for the kind of leadership that inspires trust, connection, and purpose in those around you.

Setting a Vision for Yourself

Embarking on your leadership journey can feel overwhelming at times. With so many responsibilities to juggle—tasks to complete, people to guide, goals to meet—it's easy to feel pulled in countless directions. That's why setting a personal vision is one of the most empowering steps you can take as a leader. A personal vision is more than a set of objectives; it's your anchor. It defines the kind of leader you want to be, the impact you aim to create, and the legacy you hope to leave behind.

While organizational goals are important, a personal vision goes deeper. It's about aligning your leadership with your core values and aspirations. It ensures that no matter how hectic things get, you remain grounded in what truly matters to you. Your vision is the lens through which you make decisions, face challenges, and inspire others. It's not just about what you do— it's about why you do it.

A clear and compelling vision gives your leadership clarity and purpose. It keeps you connected to the bigger picture, even when the day-to-day demands threaten to obscure it. As a new leader, it's easy to get caught up in the details, losing sight of the broader impact you're working toward. Your vision serves as a constant reminder of your long-term goals, motivating you to navigate challenges with resilience and intention.

More importantly, vision is contagious. When you lead with purpose, it resonates with others. People want to follow leaders who have a clear sense of direction—who know where they're going and why it matters. Your vision becomes a rallying point, inspiring your team to align their efforts with a shared purpose.

Having a personal vision also shifts you from being reactive to being proactive. Without a vision, it's easy to feel like you're constantly responding to what's in front of you—putting out fires, solving immediate problems, checking off tasks. But when you have a vision, you lead with intention. Each decision you make, each action you take, is aligned with your greater purpose. This proactive approach helps you anticipate challenges, adapt with confidence, and create meaningful progress.

So how do you define your vision? Start by asking yourself big, meaningful questions: What kind of leader do I want to be? What values do I want to embody? What impact do I want to leave on my team, my organization, and even the world? Let your answers guide you. Your vision doesn't have to be perfect or final—it can evolve as you grow—but it should reflect what truly matters to you.

Once you've defined your vision, write it down. Make it tangible. Refer to it often, especially during challenging moments. Let it guide your decisions, fuel your motivation, and keep you focused on the leader you're striving to become.

With a personal vision, leadership becomes more than just managing tasks or meeting goals. It becomes a purposeful journey—a chance to create something lasting, meaningful, and uniquely yours.

Before crafting your vision, it's essential to define your personal goals as a leader. These goals serve as the foundation for the impact you want to create, both in your role and within your team. Start by reflecting on questions like: What do I want my team to achieve under my leadership? How do I want to be remembered as a leader? What values will guide my decisions and actions? Your answers will shape the qualities you want to embody and the outcomes you strive to achieve.

Your goals should encompass both tangible and intangible elements. Tangible goals might include improving productivity, completing key projects, or achieving performance milestones. Intangible goals, on the other hand, are about the culture you want to create—fostering collaboration, building trust, or inspiring innovation. By blending these two types of goals, you set a course for not only driving measurable results but also creating a meaningful experience for your team. This balance ensures that your leadership isn't just about getting things done but about making a lasting, positive impact.

A personal vision is deeply individual, but its strength lies in its ability to connect with a larger purpose. As a leader, your role isn't just about pursuing your own goals—it's about advancing the mission of your organization. Aligning your vision with organizational priorities demonstrates your commitment to the team's shared success and reinforces the trust of your team and supervisors alike.

For example, if your organization emphasizes customer

satisfaction, your personal vision might include improving how your team interacts with clients or enhancing processes that directly affect the customer experience. This alignment shows that you're not just focused on your own aspirations—you're intentionally working to elevate the organization as a whole.

When your vision aligns with the company's mission, it serves as a unifying force. It connects your personal values with the broader goals of the organization, creating clarity and purpose in your decision-making. This alignment also makes it easier to gain buy-in from your team, as they see that your leadership is driven by both personal integrity and a shared purpose.

Creating a vision statement is one of the most powerful steps you can take to define your leadership journey. It's your chance to articulate your purpose in a way that resonates with both your heart and your actions. A great vision statement doesn't have to be lengthy or complicated. In fact, simplicity often carries the most impact. The goal is to distill what you stand for as a leader, what you hope to accomplish, and the kind of impact you want to have—all in a few sentences.

For example, a vision statement might look like this:

"I strive to create a culture of trust, collaboration, and innovation, where every team member feels valued and empowered to contribute to meaningful goals."

Or this:

"My purpose is to lead with authenticity and empathy, inspire growth, and foster an environment where people can thrive both individually and collectively."

Your vision statement should feel personal. It's not about creating a lofty aspiration to impress others; it's about crafting something that inspires and grounds you. Think of it as a commitment—to yourself, your team, and the values you want to embody as a leader. This isn't just about what you want to achieve but also about how you want to lead and the legacy you hope to leave.

Once your vision is in place, let it guide everything you do. Leadership can feel like a whirlwind of competing demands, and it's easy to get pulled in different directions. Your vision becomes your compass, helping you stay focused on what truly matters. When faced with tough decisions, pause and ask yourself: Does this align with my vision? Will this action reflect the leader I aspire to be?

This alignment is what keeps you grounded. It ensures that your choices are intentional, driven by purpose rather than circumstance. Over time, this consistency builds trust—not just within your team but also within yourself.

Your vision is also a tool for growth. As you gain experience and encounter new challenges, revisit your vision regularly. Reflect on whether your actions align with your stated goals. Ask yourself: *Am I living up to this vision? Does this vision still reflect the leader I'm becoming?*

A vision isn't static; it evolves as you do. This evolution is a sign of growth, a testament to your journey as a leader. Embrace the changes. They're evidence of deeper understanding and a commitment to continual improvement.

Your vision is more than words on a page—it's the essence of who you are as a leader. Let it guide you, inspire you, and remind you of the meaningful impact you're here to create.

A strong personal vision doesn't just guide you—it has the power to inspire your team. When you're deeply connected to your purpose, that passion becomes contagious. People are naturally drawn to leaders who believe in something bigger than themselves, and your vision provides a powerful rallying point. The key is to share it in a way that resonates with your team and encourages them to engage with it.

You don't need to share your vision statement word for word. Instead, bring it to life by embodying its values and goals in your actions. For instance, if your vision emphasizes open communication, create opportunities for open dialogue—

whether through team meetings, one-on-one check-ins, or collaborative brainstorming sessions. Let your commitment to transparency and inclusivity shine in how you lead.

Inspiring your team with your vision starts with how you show up every day. Leadership isn't about telling people what to do—it's about showing them what's possible. When your actions align with your vision, it demonstrates that you're not just talking about values like trust, collaboration, or innovation—you're living them.

This kind of authenticity builds credibility. When your team sees that you're genuinely invested in the purpose and goals you've set, they're more likely to feel motivated and aligned with those same objectives. Leadership is about creating a sense of shared purpose. When your team feels connected to that purpose, they're more likely to bring their best energy, creativity, and effort to the table.

Building Trust and Credibility

Why Trust is Essential in Leadership

In any leadership role, trust isn't just an advantage—it's the foundation on which everything else is built. Without trust, even the most well-thought-out strategies, exceptional communication skills, or sound decisions can fall short. But with trust, a team becomes more than just a group of individuals—it becomes a unified force driven by shared purpose and mutual respect.

As a new leader, building trust with your team may be one of the most critical and impactful tasks you undertake. Trust is what allows collaboration to flourish, motivation to thrive, and goals to be pursued with commitment. Without it, team members may disengage, communication breaks down, and even the simplest tasks can feel like uphill battles.

So what does trust mean in the context of leadership? At its core, trust is the confidence your team has in you—confidence in your integrity, your intentions, and your ability to lead them effectively. Trust isn't something you can demand or assume; it has to be earned, one interaction at a time. Every decision, every conversation, and every response you give is an opportunity to either strengthen or diminish that trust. Early in your leadership journey, focusing intentionally on earning trust will create a foundation that supports you and your team through challenges and successes alike.

When a team trusts its leader, something powerful happens: they feel safe. This sense of psychological safety is what enables team members to take risks, share ideas, and voice concerns without fear of judgment or retaliation. It's in this environment that creativity and innovation thrive. A trusted leader fosters a culture where mistakes are seen as opportunities to learn, communication flows openly, and everyone feels respected and valued.

Trust transforms how a team operates. When team members feel confident in their leader, they're more likely to engage fully, collaborate effectively, and support one another. They take ownership of their roles and align their efforts toward shared goals, creating a resilient and motivated dynamic.

Now, imagine the opposite—a team led by someone they don't trust. In such a scenario, individuals are more likely to withhold ideas, avoid taking accountability, and hesitate to provide honest feedback. The flow of information slows, morale dips, and the team's productivity suffers. Trust isn't just a "nice-to-have"; it's essential to creating an environment where everyone can do their best work.

As a leader, earning trust isn't about grand gestures or quick fixes—it's about consistent actions that align with your words. Show integrity by following through on commitments. Be transparent, especially during tough conversations. Listen actively, showing your team that their voices matter.

Trust is built over time but can be lost in an instant. That's why it requires ongoing attention and care. When your team knows they can rely on you—not just to lead them, but to support them—they'll respond in kind. They'll trust you not just as their leader, but as someone who genuinely values their contributions and wants to see them succeed.

Trust is the foundation for every great team. And as a leader, it's the most valuable currency you'll ever have.

Trust doesn't come from likeability alone—it's rooted in credibility and integrity. Credibility is about demonstrating that you're capable, knowledgeable, and thoughtful in your role as a leader. It's built through your actions: following through on commitments, making informed decisions, and having the humility to admit when you don't have all the answers. Integrity, on the other hand, is about being consistent, honest, and principled. It's about showing up as a leader who treats everyone with respect and holds themselves to the same standards they expect from others.

A team's trust in their leader grows when they see both credibility and integrity in action. Competence shows that you're equipped to guide the team, while integrity proves that you're guiding them with purpose and fairness. Together, these qualities form the foundation of genuine trust—trust that isn't just earned but sustained.

To build credibility, prioritize transparency. When making decisions, especially those that impact your team, explain your rationale openly. Share the factors you considered, and if the decision was difficult, acknowledge that. Transparency doesn't mean sharing every detail—it means showing your team that you respect them enough to keep them informed and engaged. This openness fosters trust because it shows that you value their role in the team's journey and that your actions are aligned with their best interests.

Consistency is the quiet, steady force that underpins trust. It's what tells your team that they can rely on you—not just occasionally, but every day. This doesn't mean being rigid or unchanging; it means being dependable in how you show up and in your commitment to your values and principles. When your actions consistently align with your words, your team knows what to expect. This predictability creates a stable environment where people feel safe to contribute their best.

For instance, if you commit to regular one-on-one check-ins with your team but frequently cancel or reschedule, that inconsistency can erode trust. It sends the message, however unintentionally, that their time and concerns are not a priority. Consistency isn't about being perfect—it's about being dependable. It's about showing up, following through on your promises, and demonstrating that you're as committed to their success as you are to your own.

Over time, this steady approach becomes the backbone of trust. It signals to your team that you're not only reliable but also invested in their well-being. Consistency reinforces your credibility and integrity, proving that your leadership is grounded in both competence and care. And that, more than anything, is what builds trust that lasts.

The true test of trust comes during the most challenging moments—times of uncertainty, high stakes, or difficult decisions. As a leader, these moments can feel uncomfortable, even vulnerable. Yet it's precisely in these situations that trust is either strengthened or weakened. Maintaining trust during difficult times requires courage, honesty, and accountability.

When things don't go as planned—a missed deadline, a project setback, or even a personal misstep—transparency is essential. Admitting mistakes or acknowledging challenges isn't a sign of weakness; it's a sign of integrity. It shows your team that you value honesty over self-preservation and that you're willing to be vulnerable for the good of the group. Vulnerability, when paired with accountability, reinforces trust because it demonstrates that you're human, self-aware, and committed to doing what's right.

Difficult situations also require making tough decisions. Leaders who avoid hard choices to maintain popularity risk losing credibility. Trust doesn't mean always saying what people want to hear—it means being decisive while showing empathy. When a hard decision needs to be made, explain your reasoning, listen to your team's concerns, and acknowledge the impact on them. This approach may not result in unanimous agreement, but it builds respect and demonstrates that you're committed to leading with both integrity and care.

Trust isn't something you build once and then check off your list—it's a living, breathing part of every interaction. Each conversation, decision, and gesture either reinforces or erodes trust. That's why building trust requires ongoing effort and attention to detail.

Start small. Showing appreciation for a team member's effort, seeking honest feedback, or responding thoughtfully to concerns may seem insignificant, but these actions add up. Over time, they create a foundation of trust that grows stronger with each positive interaction. Consistency in your words and actions is key—your team needs to know they can count on you, no matter the circumstances.

As a new leader, understand that trust is a process. It can't be rushed or forced, but it can be nurtured through genuine, consistent behavior. Focus on being transparent, listening actively, and staying true to your values. When your team sees that you're committed to their well-being and to leading with integrity, trust will naturally follow.

Trust is more than a leadership asset—it's the foundation on which everything else is built. It enables collaboration, fosters resilience, and creates a sense of safety that allows teams to thrive, even in the face of adversity. By prioritizing trust, especially in difficult situations, you position yourself as a leader your team can rely on—someone who doesn't shy away from challenges but faces them with courage, honesty, and care.

Over time, trust becomes the bedrock of your leadership. With it, you can lead confidently, knowing your team stands with you, ready to face whatever comes next together.

Developing Trust through Transparency

Transparency is at the heart of trust in leadership. When leaders are open about their decisions, intentions, and even challenges, they create an environment where team members feel valued, included, and respected. Transparency doesn't mean sharing every detail or thought—it's about providing enough insight into your reasoning to make your team feel like active participants in the journey. For new leaders, embracing transparency is a powerful way to build trust, establish credibility, and foster a culture of open communication and collaboration.

Transparent leaders bring clarity. They explain the why behind their decisions, giving team members a sense of purpose and connection to their work. When people understand how their contributions align with the team's goals, they're more likely to engage with enthusiasm and commitment. For a new leader, transparency is also a way to define your leadership identity—showing your team that you lead with integrity, empathy, and a genuine desire to include them in the process.

One of the most impactful ways to practice transparency is through open communication about decisions. Leadership often requires making choices that directly affect your team, whether it's reallocating resources, adjusting timelines, or setting new priorities. Instead of simply announcing these decisions, take the extra step to explain them. Share the factors you considered, the goals you're aiming to achieve, and how the decision aligns with the team's overall mission.

For example, if you decide to reassign team members to different projects, don't just inform them of the change— share the reasoning behind it. Explain how the new assignments are designed to leverage their strengths, address specific challenges, or advance strategic goals. This approach doesn't just inform your team; it involves them. It shows that you've put thought into the decision and considered its impact on the team as a whole.

When people understand the why behind your decisions, they're more likely to trust and support them—even if the outcome isn't exactly what they would have preferred. Transparency demonstrates that you're thoughtful and intentional, that you've considered their perspectives, and that your actions are aligned with the team's best interests.

Transparency isn't just a tool for individual decisions; it's a mindset that shapes how you lead every day. Over time, consistent transparency fosters a culture of openness and mutual respect. Team members feel safe to ask questions, share feedback, and contribute ideas because they see that their leader values honesty and collaboration.

As a new leader, practicing transparency helps you create a foundation for trust and credibility. It shows your team that you're not just managing them—you're leading with integrity, clarity, and a commitment to their success. And as that trust grows, so does your ability to guide your team toward meaningful goals and lasting impact.

Transparency isn't just about celebrating successes—it's about being honest when things don't go as planned. As a leader, there will inevitably be setbacks: missed goals, shifting priorities, or unexpected challenges. In these moments, it can feel tempting to maintain a polished, in-control image. But the reality is, acknowledging challenges doesn't weaken your authority—it strengthens your credibility.

When you're open about obstacles, your team sees that you're willing to be real with them. This honesty fosters trust and connection, showing that you're not hiding behind a façade but facing the difficulties alongside them. For example, if a project is running behind schedule due to unforeseen issues, communicate this openly. Explain the situation, outline the steps you're taking to address it, and invite input from the team. This collaborative approach turns a challenge into an opportunity for collective problem-solving and reinforces that you value their perspectives.

More importantly, being transparent about challenges demonstrates resilience. It shows your team that setbacks are part of the journey—and that what matters most is how you respond. By addressing difficulties constructively, you set a powerful example of how to handle adversity with grace and determination.

While transparency is essential to building trust, not everything can or should be shared. As a leader, you'll encounter situations—such as personnel decisions, sensitive financial data, or strategic plans—that require discretion. Balancing transparency with confidentiality is a key part of leading with integrity and professionalism.

The goal is to share as much as you can without compromising the boundaries of your role. If there's information you can't disclose, be honest about it. Let your team know that certain details must remain confidential but that you're committed to keeping them informed wherever possible. This approach shows respect for both transparency and the need for discretion, reinforcing your credibility as a thoughtful and ethical leader.

For example, you might say: *"I can't share all the details right now, but here's what I can tell you..."* This kind of communication reassures your team that while you're mindful of organizational needs, you're also committed to keeping them in the loop.

Being transparent about challenges and balancing that with confidentiality creates a leadership style rooted in trust and integrity. It shows your team that you're honest, even in difficult times, and that you respect the boundaries required to protect the organization's interests.

Over time, this balance builds credibility. Your team comes to see you as someone they can rely on—not just to share the good news, but to navigate the tough moments with clarity, honesty, and professionalism. This level of trust becomes a cornerstone of your leadership, enabling you to lead with confidence and authenticity, no matter what challenges arise.

Creating a transparent environment isn't just about sharing information—it's about building a culture where openness, trust, and collaboration thrive. Transparency encourages team members to feel comfortable sharing their ideas, concerns, and feedback. When they see that you're open about your decisions and honest about both successes and challenges, they're more likely to do the same. This openness reduces misunderstandings, strengthens relationships, and fosters a sense of unity within the team.

Transparency also drives accountability—both for you and your team. When decisions, goals, and actions are visible, it naturally encourages everyone to stay aligned and take ownership of their contributions. In a transparent environment, team members have the context they need to make informed decisions, which empowers them to be more proactive and engaged in their work.

Most importantly, transparency builds trust. When your team feels that you're honest, consistent, and respectful of their need for information, they develop a deeper sense of loyalty and commitment. They see that you're leading with integrity, which makes them more likely to support you—even when the road gets tough.

Incorporating transparency into your leadership doesn't have to be complicated. It's about small, intentional actions that demonstrate your commitment to openness.

Start with regular check-ins. These moments provide an opportunity to share updates on goals, discuss challenges, and celebrate wins. During meetings, make space for questions and actively encourage your team to share their insights. If a decision is in progress and not yet finalized, let your team know where things stand. Even saying, "Here's what we know so far, and I'll update you as soon as I have more details," reinforces your commitment to keeping them informed.

Another powerful way to practice transparency is by seeking feedback. Ask your team: Do you feel informed? Are there areas where you'd like more clarity? This simple step not only helps you refine your communication but also shows your team that you value their perspectives.

Transparency isn't about perfection—it's about consistency. By openly sharing the why behind decisions, encouraging dialogue, and being honest about what you do and don't know, you create an environment where trust and mutual respect can flourish.

A transparent environment is more than just a leadership style—it's a culture. It fosters trust, strengthens relationships, and empowers your team to work together toward shared goals. By practicing transparency daily, you set the tone for how your team communicates, collaborates, and thrives.

Over time, these small, intentional acts of transparency become the foundation for a leadership legacy built on trust and integrity—one that inspires others to lead with openness and purpose as well.

Consistency and Integrity

As a leader, your words and actions are constantly being observed. Your team looks to you for guidance, gauging your reliability and commitment through the decisions you make and the way you carry yourself. Consistency and integrity are the bedrock of that trust. While trust is earned over time, it can be lost in an instant through inconsistent behavior or broken promises.

To lead with consistency and integrity means showing up authentically, following through on your commitments, and aligning your actions with your stated values. It's about being someone your team can count on—not just when things are going well, but especially when circumstances are challenging. When your actions reflect your principles, you create a foundation of trust that strengthens your leadership and inspires loyalty.

Consistency is one of the most underrated yet essential qualities of effective leadership. It provides stability, creating an environment where team members feel secure in your leadership. When people know they can rely on you to act in a steady and predictable way, they can focus on their work without unnecessary distractions or uncertainty. This sense of security fosters collaboration, engagement, and productivity.

Consistency also reinforces your credibility. For example, if you set expectations for punctuality or meeting deadlines, your team is far more likely to respect those standards if they see you consistently upholding them. On the other hand, inconsistency—such as setting rules you don't follow or failing to deliver on promises—undermines your credibility and creates confusion. When trust wavers, so does team morale and cohesion.

For new leaders, establishing consistency early is critical. It sets the tone for the kind of environment you want to build. Every action, no matter how small, is an opportunity to demonstrate that your words and values align with your behavior.

Consistency doesn't mean rigidity. Leadership often requires adaptability—responding to change, making quick decisions, and pivoting when necessary. The key is to remain adaptable without losing your grounding in core values, priorities, and goals. Consistency and adaptability can coexist. You can adjust your methods and strategies to meet changing circumstances while maintaining a steady commitment to what truly matters.

For example, if unforeseen circumstances require you to adjust a deadline, communicate the why clearly and transparently. Show your team that while external factors may shift, your dedication to fairness, quality, and accountability remains the same. This balance between adaptability and consistency demonstrates resilience and reliability—two qualities that inspire confidence in your leadership.

Consistency and integrity aren't just leadership qualities—they're commitments. They show your team that you're not only capable of leading them but that you're someone who respects and values their trust. By consistently aligning your actions with your values, you build a legacy of reliability and authenticity.

In the end, leadership isn't about perfection. It's about showing up—steadily, authentically, and with purpose. When you lead with consistency and integrity, you create a foundation of trust that empowers your team to do their best work, knowing they can rely on you every step of the way.

Integrity is more than just doing the right thing—it's about consistently acting in alignment with your values, especially when it's inconvenient or difficult. Leaders who lead with integrity earn respect because their actions reflect a deep commitment to honesty, fairness, and ethical behavior. Integrity becomes especially important in tough situations, such as making unpopular decisions, delivering difficult feedback, or resolving conflicts. When you approach these moments with integrity, your team sees that you prioritize their well-being, the team's values, and the organization's mission over personal gain.

Being a leader with integrity starts with transparency and honesty. It means acknowledging when things haven't gone as planned, taking responsibility for mistakes, and avoiding blame-shifting. While admitting mistakes may feel vulnerable, it demonstrates courage and builds trust. Team members value a leader who owns up to errors rather than covering them up or deflecting responsibility. Integrity also means treating everyone with respect and fairness—ensuring that each person's contributions are recognized and valued.

Leaders who act with integrity don't just fulfill their roles— they inspire loyalty. When your team sees that you operate with honesty and fairness, they're more likely to reciprocate with trust, respect, and commitment. Integrity isn't just a quality of effective leadership; it's the foundation of a culture where people feel safe, supported, and empowered to do their best work.

Leadership requires constant decision-making, from day-to-day choices to high-stakes challenges. Consistency and integrity serve as a moral compass, guiding these decisions in a way that reflects your values and builds trust. When you base decisions on your core values and communicate those values openly, your team understands the principles driving your actions. This transparency reassures them that your decisions are rooted in fairness and integrity.

In situations where priorities compete, consistency in your decision-making process becomes critical. For instance, if one of your core values is fostering team growth, your decisions should consistently reflect that—whether by providing learning opportunities, offering constructive feedback, or encouraging team members to take on challenging projects. When your team sees that you prioritize their development, they'll trust your decisions, even if they don't always agree with every choice.

Leading with integrity also requires looking beyond short-term gains to consider long-term consequences. While it may be tempting to cut corners to meet an immediate deadline, doing so can harm morale, quality, or your team's trust. Integrity means choosing the path that aligns with your values, even when it's more difficult or takes more time. For example, if meeting a tight deadline would compromise quality, integrity might involve renegotiating timelines or reallocating resources to maintain standards.

By leading with consistency and integrity, you create a leadership legacy built on trust and respect. It's not just about making the right decisions; it's about showing your team that you're committed to doing what's right, no matter the circumstances.

Integrity is one of the most enduring qualities of effective leadership. It demonstrates accountability to your role, commitment to your values, and care for the people you lead. When your actions consistently align with your principles, you inspire trust and loyalty that lasts long after individual decisions are made.

Leading with integrity isn't always easy, but it's always worth it. It's the difference between leading by authority and leading by example—and the latter is what creates meaningful, lasting impact.

The alignment between your actions and words is the foundation of trust. When you commit to something, follow through. When you set standards, apply them consistently—not just to your team but to yourself. This alignment reinforces your credibility and shows that you respect your commitments and hold yourself to the same expectations as everyone else.

Your team is always observing. If you emphasize the importance of punctuality but regularly arrive late to meetings, the inconsistency can create confusion and frustration. However, when you model the behaviors and attitudes you expect, your team is more likely to follow suit. Leading by example isn't just about setting the tone—it's about demonstrating accountability. It shows your team that you're not only willing to hold them accountable but also to hold yourself accountable.

Occasional slip-ups are inevitable—we're all human. When they happen, acknowledge them openly. Apologize if needed, and take steps to make things right. These moments of honesty and humility strengthen trust because they show self-awareness and a commitment to continuous improvement.

Consistency and integrity aren't just for major decisions or high-stakes situations—they're qualities to be practiced every day. It's the small, consistent actions you take that shape the culture of your team. For example, consistently thanking team members for their efforts fosters a culture of appreciation. Taking the time to listen to their concerns builds a culture of respect. These seemingly small gestures compound over time, creating a team dynamic rooted in trust and collaboration.

To keep integrity and consistency top of mind, consider starting each day with a moment of reflection. Ask yourself: What kind of leader do I want to be today? How can I show up in a way that aligns with my values? Setting these intentions helps you stay grounded, even when unexpected challenges arise.

Remember, consistency doesn't mean rigidity. Leadership often requires flexibility, but your adaptability should always be anchored in your values. By staying true to your principles while navigating change, you show your team that you're both steady and responsive.

When you consistently align your actions with your words, you create an environment of trust and security. Team members feel respected, valued, and confident in their roles because they know what to expect from you. They see that you're not just leading them—you're leading with them.

This daily commitment to integrity and consistency sets the tone for a culture where everyone feels empowered to bring their best. It's not about perfection; it's about showing up authentically and reliably, day after day. Over time, this creates a foundation of trust that enables your team to thrive and your leadership to inspire.

The Power of Vulnerability

Vulnerability in leadership is often misunderstood. Many new leaders feel compelled to project an image of unwavering confidence, control, and competence, as though admitting uncertainty might undermine their authority. But true leadership isn't about perfection—it's about being human. It's about showing up as your authentic self, flaws and all, to create a space where others feel safe to do the same. Vulnerability, when embraced wisely, is a powerful tool for building trust, inspiring loyalty, and fostering connection.

Being vulnerable as a leader doesn't mean oversharing or appearing unguarded in ways that might cause discomfort. Instead, it's about having the courage to be real. It's about acknowledging when you don't have all the answers, asking for help when needed, and owning up to mistakes without letting ego get in the way. When you show vulnerability, you model authenticity, creating a culture where your team feels empowered to take risks, share ideas, and fully engage.

Vulnerability is the foundation of genuine connection, and connection is at the heart of effective leadership. When you share your struggles, uncertainties, or lessons learned with your team, you bridge the gap between leader and team member. You remind them that leadership isn't about being infallible—it's about being willing to grow and learn alongside them.

In a culture that values vulnerability, team members feel psychologically safe to express themselves openly, knowing they won't be judged or dismissed. This sense of safety encourages better collaboration, greater innovation, and stronger resilience. People are more likely to share ideas, offer unique perspectives, and support one another through challenges when they feel seen and heard.

For example, imagine acknowledging to your team that a decision didn't work out as planned. Instead of deflecting blame, you openly reflect on what you learned and invite the team to explore solutions together. This not only humanizes you as a leader but also fosters a spirit of collective problem-solving. It shows your team that vulnerability isn't a weakness—it's a strength.

As a new leader, vulnerability allows you to set the tone for an open, authentic team culture. It starts with small but meaningful acts: admitting when you're unsure about something, asking for feedback, or sharing a story about a time you learned from a mistake. These moments of honesty demonstrate that you're not just leading from a position of authority—you're leading with humility and authenticity.

Vulnerability also creates space for others to bring their full selves to work. When your team sees you being real, they feel permission to be real too. This kind of openness fosters trust, deepens relationships, and builds a sense of belonging.

Leadership isn't about always having the right answers—it's about creating an environment where people feel safe enough to find the answers together. When you lead with vulnerability, you unlock the potential for meaningful connection, stronger collaboration, and a resilient, engaged team.

Vulnerability is not a liability—it's an asset. It's the courage to say, I'm still learning, and that's okay. It's the willingness to connect with your team on a human level, showing them that leadership isn't about being perfect—it's about being present, honest, and committed to growth.

By embracing vulnerability, you create a culture of authenticity and trust where your team can thrive. It's in these spaces of openness that the best ideas emerge, the strongest bonds form, and the greatest resilience is built. And as you lead with vulnerability, you'll find that the connections you create aren't just beneficial for your team—they'll transform you as a leader as well.

Mistakes are an inevitable part of leadership and growth. As a leader, how you handle those moments speaks volumes about your character and leadership style. One of the simplest yet most impactful ways to demonstrate vulnerability is by admitting your mistakes. When you own your missteps openly, you model humility, self-awareness, and a commitment to learning—all qualities that inspire trust and respect.

Admitting mistakes doesn't weaken your authority—it strengthens it. It shows your team that you're human, accountable, and willing to grow. For example, if a project deadline is missed due to an oversight, don't sweep it under the rug. Instead, address it with your team. Share what you've learned and invite them to contribute ideas on how to avoid similar issues in the future. This approach doesn't just resolve the immediate problem—it also fosters a culture of openness and continuous improvement.

By normalizing mistakes as learning opportunities, you encourage your team to approach challenges with curiosity and resilience rather than fear or defensiveness. This practice cultivates a growth mindset where everyone feels safe taking risks, learning from setbacks, and striving for improvement together.

Another powerful way to demonstrate vulnerability is by asking for help. Leaders often feel pressure to have all the answers, but the truth is, leadership isn't about knowing everything—it's about creating an environment where collaboration thrives. When you ask for help or seek input from your team, you show respect for their skills, perspectives, and expertise. Far from undermining your leadership, this openness builds trust and reinforces your team's sense of value and purpose.

Inviting input also has tangible benefits. Team members who feel involved in the decision-making process are more invested in the outcomes. By tapping into their collective knowledge, you're more likely to arrive at creative, well-rounded solutions. At the same time, involving the team fosters a sense of ownership and unity, where decisions are seen as a collaborative effort rather than the leader's responsibility alone.

For instance, if you're navigating a complex strategic decision and feel uncertain about the best course of action, be honest with your team. Say something like, *"I'd love to hear your thoughts on this. Your insights are invaluable, and I want to make sure we're approaching this from every angle."* This simple act of vulnerability builds trust, encourages dialogue, and often leads to better decisions.

Embracing vulnerability—whether by owning mistakes or asking for help—creates an atmosphere of authenticity and trust. It shows your team that leadership isn't about perfection; it's about showing up honestly, learning together, and working as a united team toward shared goals.

When leaders model this openness, they foster a culture where mistakes are embraced as opportunities to grow, collaboration is celebrated, and everyone feels empowered to contribute their best. Vulnerability isn't a sign of weakness—it's a hallmark of courageous and impactful leadership.

Vulnerability isn't just about sharing your own experiences— it's also about recognizing and empathizing with the challenges your team faces. Leadership is as much about understanding as it is about guiding. Acknowledging the struggles, frustrations, and stressors that your team members encounter shows that you genuinely care about their well-being and success. By demonstrating empathy, you create stronger connections and foster an environment where team members feel comfortable bringing their whole selves to work.

For example, if a team member is grappling with a heavy

workload or a difficult project, take a moment to acknowledge the difficulty. You don't have to solve the problem for them—sometimes, the most impactful thing you can do is let them know you see their effort and appreciate their resilience. A simple statement like, "I know this has been a tough week, and I see how hard you're working to get through it," can go a long way in making someone feel valued and understood.

These small, consistent acts of empathy build trust, respect, and cohesion within the team. They show your team that you're not just focused on outcomes but also on the people driving them. When individuals feel respected and understood, they're more likely to stay engaged, collaborate effectively, and contribute their best.

While vulnerability is a powerful tool, it must be balanced with authority and confidence. Leadership requires guiding your team through challenges, making tough decisions, and maintaining stability even in uncertain times. Vulnerability doesn't mean downplaying your leadership role—it means showing enough openness to connect with your team while remaining confident in your ability to lead.

When sharing vulnerabilities, focus on the lessons learned or the path forward rather than dwelling on uncertainty or self-doubt. For instance, if you're navigating a complex decision, you might say: "This is a challenging situation, and while I don't have all the answers yet, I'm confident that, together, we'll find the best path forward." This approach acknowledges the challenge while demonstrating resolve, showing your team that you value their input and trust their capabilities.

It's also important to keep personal vulnerabilities in check, ensuring that what you share remains relevant to your role and the team's success. The goal isn't to offload emotional burdens onto your team but to create a space of trust and authenticity. Sharing appropriately and professionally allows you to foster connection without undermining your authority or overstepping boundaries.

Balancing vulnerability with authority is what allows leaders to inspire trust, build relationships, and guide their teams effectively. When you empathize with your team's challenges, you show that you care about them as individuals, not just as contributors to a goal. And when you combine this empathy with confidence and clear direction, you create a dynamic where trust and respect thrive.

Leadership isn't about being perfect—it's about being human. It's about showing that you're willing to listen, learn, and grow alongside your team. By embracing vulnerability while maintaining your authority, you set the tone for a culture of openness, trust, and mutual respect that enables your team to succeed and thrive.

The ultimate goal of vulnerability in leadership is to create a team culture where openness and authenticity are not just encouraged—they're the norm. When your team sees you leading with vulnerability, they feel empowered to do the same. It sends a clear message: Here, it's safe to be human.

Encourage your team members to share their challenges, ask for help, and view mistakes as opportunities for growth. Let them know that their honesty matters and that their voices are valued—whether they're celebrating successes, offering feedback, or expressing concerns. This openness doesn't just strengthen individual connections; it builds a collective spirit of trust and mutual respect.

A culture of vulnerability is a culture of belonging. It's a place where people feel seen, supported, and valued—not just for their achievements but for who they are. When team members know they'll be met with empathy rather than judgment, they're more willing to take risks, share ideas, and give their best.

For example, when someone admits they're struggling with a project or asks for feedback on their work, respond with understanding and encouragement. Acknowledge their courage in speaking up, and work with them to find a way forward. These moments of connection show your team that it's okay to be imperfect and that support is always available.

Belonging isn't just about feeling safe; it's about feeling connected. When your team experiences this connection, they become more motivated and resilient, ready to tackle challenges together. Vulnerability creates a foundation for collaboration and innovation because it allows people to show up authentically, without fear of judgment.

Leadership isn't about projecting invulnerability—it's about fostering a culture where trust and authenticity thrive. By modeling vulnerability and creating space for your team to do the same, you unlock the potential for growth—not just for individuals but for the team as a whole.

When vulnerability becomes a shared value, trust deepens, collaboration strengthens, and resilience flourishes. Mistakes are no longer setbacks but stepping stones. Challenges become opportunities for collective problem-solving. Success is celebrated as a shared achievement.

Cultivating a culture of vulnerability isn't just about creating a better workplace; it's about creating a better team. One where everyone feels empowered to grow, supported to succeed, and inspired to bring their best. As you lead with vulnerability, you don't just guide your team—you grow with them, forging a culture that thrives on trust, connection, and shared purpose.

Maintaining Trust in Difficult Situations

Leadership isn't truly tested during smooth sailing; it's in the moments of difficulty and uncertainty that its strength is revealed. Whether it's a project that's gone off course, unexpected organizational changes, or a high-stakes decision, these challenges expose the depth of trust between a leader and their team. In such moments, maintaining trust becomes paramount. Your team looks to you for guidance, stability, and honesty.

Upholding trust in tough times requires courage, transparency, empathy, and a steadfast commitment to acting in the team's best interest—even when the path forward isn't clear. A trusted leader reassures their team, showing them that they're not alone in facing these challenges. By approaching these moments with integrity and openness, you not only navigate the situation effectively but also deepen the trust and loyalty of your team.

In challenging times, transparency often feels like a risk. The temptation to withhold information may come from a desire to protect the team or preserve morale. While well-intentioned, this approach often backfires. People sense when something is off, and a lack of communication can lead to speculation, uncertainty, and mistrust—creating anxiety far worse than the truth itself.

Honesty is the antidote. Be upfront about the situation, even if it means acknowledging uncertainties. Share what you know, explain the steps being taken to address the issue, and, if possible, outline a timeline for when more information will become available. Honesty doesn't mean sharing every detail; it means providing enough context for your team to feel informed, respected, and included.

For example, if a project is at risk of delay due to unforeseen complications, address the situation head-on. You might say:

"We've encountered some challenges with this project that could push back our timeline. Here's what we know so far, and here's what we're doing to resolve it. I'll keep you updated as we learn more, and together, we'll adjust our approach to stay on track."

This kind of transparency shows your team that you respect them enough to keep them in the loop and trust them to handle the reality of the situation. By involving them in the problem-solving process, you transform a challenge into an opportunity for collaboration and resilience.

In times of difficulty, trust is your greatest asset. It allows your team to stay focused, collaborative, and committed even in the face of uncertainty. Transparency and honesty aren't just strategies—they're commitments that reinforce the foundation of trust you've built.

When you lead with openness and integrity, you show your team that no matter how challenging the circumstances, you're in it together. This reassurance strengthens their confidence in you and inspires their willingness to follow your lead, even when the path ahead is unclear.

Leadership in adversity is not about having all the answers—it's about showing up with honesty, empathy, and a commitment to move forward together. By doing so, you don't just navigate tough times—you emerge from them with a stronger, more connected team.

Difficult situations impact everyone differently, and as a leader, it's essential to acknowledge and empathize with your team's emotions. Uncertainty can evoke feelings of anxiety, frustration, or even demotivation. Demonstrating empathy doesn't mean solving every problem or having all the answers—it's about creating space for people to feel heard and understood.

Take time to listen. When team members share their concerns, acknowledge their feelings without minimizing them. For example, during a period of organizational restructuring, people may feel anxious about potential changes to their roles or responsibilities. Encourage open discussions, invite them to share their thoughts, and provide reassurance where possible. You might say:

"I know this transition is bringing up a lot of uncertainty, and that can be difficult. I want to make sure you feel supported, so please share

any concerns you have. We'll work through this together."

Empathy doesn't eliminate challenges, but it builds resilience within the team. It shows that you care about their well-being and creates a supportive atmosphere where people feel safe to express themselves and tackle challenges collaboratively. This culture of understanding strengthens trust and deepens the connection between leader and team.

In tough situations, mistakes happen—it's part of being human. As a leader, the way you handle mistakes can either strengthen or weaken trust. Taking responsibility for errors, rather than deflecting blame, demonstrates accountability, maturity, and a commitment to growth. Owning your mistakes doesn't diminish your authority; it enhances your credibility by prioritizing honesty and learning over self-preservation.

For instance, if a project falls short of its goals due to a planning oversight, acknowledge your role openly. Say something like:

"This didn't turn out the way we'd hoped, and I realize there were gaps in how we approached the planning. Here's what I've learned from this experience and how I'll adjust moving forward. Let's use this as a team to explore how we can improve together."

This level of accountability sets the tone for the team. When you take ownership of your actions, you encourage your team to do the same, creating a culture where mistakes are viewed as opportunities to learn and improve rather than something to hide or avoid.

Taking responsibility also means acting on the commitments you make to address mistakes. If you've outlined corrective steps, follow through with consistency and integrity. For example, if you've promised to improve planning processes, ensure those changes are implemented and communicated clearly to your team.

When leaders follow through on their commitments, it reinforces trust. It shows your team that your words are backed by action and that you're committed to continuous improvement—not just in the moment but for the long term. This builds confidence in your leadership, especially during difficult times, by demonstrating that you're dependable and focused on solutions.

Leadership during challenging times requires a blend of empathy and accountability. By listening to your team, acknowledging their concerns, and showing genuine care for their well-being, you create an environment of trust and resilience. By taking responsibility for mistakes and following through on commitments, you model the kind of integrity and ownership that inspires your team to do the same.

In the end, leadership isn't about avoiding challenges—it's about navigating them with authenticity, humility, and a commitment to growth. By demonstrating empathy and accountability, you foster a team culture that thrives on trust, collaboration, and shared purpose, no matter the obstacles.

In challenging times, your team looks to you for guidance and reassurance. They want to know that despite the obstacles, you have a plan and the confidence to see it through. While it's natural to feel stress in these moments, maintaining a calm and steady demeanor helps your team stay focused and grounded. This doesn't mean ignoring your emotions or pretending everything is fine—it's about channeling your resilience and demonstrating composure.

For example, if a deadline is unexpectedly moved up, your initial reaction might be stress or frustration. But by taking a moment to compose yourself and then presenting a clear plan of action, you demonstrate calm leadership. Share the new timeline, explain the adjustments to priorities, and offer support to your team as they navigate the increased workload. When your team sees you responding with a level head, they'll feel more confident in their ability to tackle the challenge alongside you.

A steady hand also requires decisiveness. Indecision in tough times can create confusion and amplify stress. Even when the path forward isn't entirely clear, make the best decision you can with the information at hand, and communicate it confidently. For example, "Here's the approach we're going to take. It may need adjustments along the way, but this is the direction we'll start with." Decisive action provides your team with a sense of direction and purpose, allowing them to focus on moving forward rather than dwelling on uncertainty.

During difficult times, it's easy for team members to lose sight of why their efforts matter. Setbacks and challenges can overshadow the bigger picture, leading to frustration or demotivation. As a leader, one of the most impactful ways to maintain trust is by reconnecting your team to their sense of purpose.

Remind your team of the mission behind their work. If a project has hit repeated obstacles, take a moment to discuss its broader impact—how it benefits the organization, serves customers, or makes a difference in the community. For example, you might say:

"I know this project has been demanding, but remember the value it's creating for our customers. What we're building will improve their lives, and that's something worth pushing through these challenges for."

Reaffirming the importance of their efforts helps your team see beyond the immediate difficulties. It shifts the focus from short-term setbacks to the meaningful impact of their work. Purpose provides motivation, helping people persevere and remain committed, even in the face of adversity.

Guiding with a steady hand and reinforcing a sense of purpose are two cornerstones of leadership during challenging times. When you approach adversity with composure, decisiveness, and clarity, you provide the stability your team needs to navigate uncertainty. And when you remind them of the greater mission behind their work, you give them a reason to stay motivated and resilient.

Leadership isn't about eliminating challenges—it's about showing your team how to rise to them. By leading with steadiness and purpose, you foster trust, inspire confidence, and keep your team aligned, no matter how difficult the path ahead may seem.

Effective Communication Skills

The Leader's Role as a Communicator

Effective communication is one of the most vital skills a leader can master. A leader's words, tone, and approach to sharing information shape not only how the team understands tasks but also how they feel about their work. Clear and purposeful communication eliminates misunderstandings, fosters collaboration, and aligns the team toward shared goals. But communication in leadership goes beyond delivering information—it's about inspiring and empowering your team to perform at their best.

The leader's role as a communicator is twofold. First, it's about articulating the team's vision, goals, and expectations with clarity and conviction. Second, it involves listening—creating a two-way dialogue that enables you to understand your team's needs, concerns, and ideas. Balancing these elements builds trust, fosters inclusion, and ensures your team feels heard and valued. When you communicate effectively, you strengthen connections, elevate morale, and enhance your overall impact as a leader.

The foundation of effective communication is clarity. As a leader, your responsibility isn't just to tell your team what to do—it's to help them understand why it matters. Providing context and connecting tasks to the bigger picture helps your team see the purpose behind their work, which drives engagement and motivation.

For example, if you're assigning a high-priority project with a tight deadline, explain why it's critical. Perhaps it's tied to delivering value to a key client or achieving an organizational milestone. By sharing the urgency and importance, you help your team feel more connected to the mission and more motivated to deliver their best effort.

Clarity is especially vital during high-pressure situations. In these moments, your ability to minimize confusion and focus the team on actionable steps is essential. Clear communication creates calm and confidence, even when the stakes are high.

Equally important is the need to be concise. Leaders often feel compelled to over-explain, but too much detail can dilute the message. Aim to communicate the essential points succinctly, leaving room for follow-up questions or discussions. A clear and direct approach not only improves understanding but also reduces the risk of misinterpretation and frustration.

Effective communication isn't just about sharing information; it's about inspiring action. When you connect your team's work to a greater purpose, you give them a reason to care beyond the immediate task. Purpose-driven communication fosters motivation and unity, transforming routine assignments into meaningful contributions to a larger mission.

Remember, communication is a two-way street. Make time to listen actively, inviting feedback and encouraging your team to share their ideas and concerns. When people feel heard, they're more likely to engage fully, contribute creatively, and stay aligned with the team's goals.

As a leader, your words have the power to guide, motivate,

and inspire. By communicating with clarity, purpose, and genuine connection, you create an environment where your team feels empowered to succeed—and where everyone thrives together.

Leadership communication goes beyond relaying information—it's about inspiring your team and engaging them in a shared vision. Words have the power to uplift, energize, and motivate people to achieve more than they thought possible. A leader who communicates with enthusiasm and purpose ignites similar energy within their team, creating a culture where individuals feel excited to contribute.

Your language and tone matter. Positive reinforcement, encouragement, and genuine expressions of appreciation foster respect and motivation. When you speak to your team, let your passion for the mission shine through. Highlight the impact of their efforts, no matter how small. For example, instead of saying, *"We met the deadline,"* try, *"Your hard work made meeting this deadline possible, and it's going to make a big difference for our client."* By framing communication with purpose and positivity, you cultivate a sense of pride and belonging that energizes your team.

Engagement is also about recognizing progress and celebrating achievements. Regularly acknowledge successes—whether it's completing a challenging project, solving a problem creatively, or simply showing consistent effort. Recognition reinforces the message that their work matters and motivates them to continue striving for excellence. It transforms a group of individuals into a cohesive team that feels valued, driven, and aligned toward shared goals.

Listening is one of the most overlooked yet essential aspects of leadership communication. It's not just about hearing words—it's about truly understanding the ideas, concerns, and perspectives your team brings to the table. Leaders who actively listen create an environment where people feel respected, valued, and safe to speak openly. This openness fosters trust, deepens relationships, and strengthens team cohesion.

Active listening involves giving your full attention, asking thoughtful questions, and responding with care. Avoid the temptation to interrupt or formulate your response while someone else is speaking. Instead, focus entirely on what's being shared. Listening isn't just about gathering information; it's about showing that you value your team's input.

For instance, if a team member raises a concern about a challenging deadline, acknowledge their perspective: *"I hear that this timeline feels tight for you. Can you share more about what's making it difficult?"* Follow up with empathy and, where possible, solutions that address their concern. This approach demonstrates that you respect their input and are committed to finding collaborative ways to move forward.

When team members see that their voices are heard and valued, it builds trust and encourages open dialogue. They become more willing to share ideas, raise concerns, and contribute creatively. Listening transforms communication from a one-way directive into a two-way partnership, reinforcing the bond between leader and team.

Inspiring, engaging, and listening are the cornerstones of effective leadership communication. When you communicate with passion and clarity, recognize progress, and listen actively, you create an environment where your team feels valued and connected to a shared purpose.

Leadership isn't just about what you say—it's about how you make your team feel. By showing enthusiasm for the mission, celebrating successes, and listening with intent, you build trust, foster collaboration, and inspire your team to reach new heights together.

Leadership communication isn't a one-way directive—it's a two-way dialogue. When you encourage your team to share ideas, voice concerns, and ask questions, you create an atmosphere of collaboration where everyone feels heard and valued. Two-way dialogue is more than just communication;

it's a bridge that connects your vision with the team's insights, ensuring alignment and fostering trust.

As a leader, make it a priority to create opportunities for this engagement. Regular check-ins, open forums, or brainstorming sessions are powerful ways to invite input and build a culture of openness. When people feel safe speaking up, they're more likely to contribute ideas that spark innovation and address challenges proactively.

For example, during team meetings, carve out space for open discussion. After presenting a new project or initiative, ask for feedback:

"What do you think about this approach? Are there any concerns or opportunities we might have missed?"

Listen attentively to each response, showing genuine interest in what's being shared. This simple act signals that everyone's opinion matters and reinforces that your team's input is essential for success. By fostering two-way communication, you not only build trust but also strengthen collaboration and ensure that decisions are informed by the collective wisdom of the group.

Effective communication isn't one-size-fits-all. Each person on your team processes information differently, and as a leader, it's your job to adapt your style to meet their needs. Flexibility in communication shows that you respect and value individual differences, which deepens your connection with your team and empowers them to perform at their best.

Pay attention to how your team members prefer to receive information. Some may thrive with clear, concise instructions, while others may need more context or detailed explanations to feel confident in their understanding. By tailoring your communication style to suit these preferences, you demonstrate empathy and create an environment where everyone feels supported.

For instance, if you're working with someone who prefers visual aids, use charts or diagrams to clarify complex ideas. If another team member values detailed explanations, take the time to provide thorough context. This adaptability requires attentiveness, but it allows you to connect with each person in a way that resonates with them.

Leaders who adapt their communication styles build stronger relationships because each team member feels seen and understood. This flexibility fosters a collaborative environment where everyone is equipped to contribute their unique strengths toward achieving the team's goals.

Fostering two-way dialogue and adapting your communication style are essential for building trust, unity, and effectiveness within your team. By encouraging open discussions and meeting people where they are, you create a culture where ideas flourish, challenges are addressed, and everyone feels valued.

Leadership isn't about having all the answers—it's about creating the conditions for your team to thrive. By embracing collaboration and flexibility in your communication, you strengthen the bonds within your team and empower them to achieve their fullest potential, together.

Active Listening for Better Results

Active listening is a dynamic process involving three key elements that help you connect with your team on a meaningful level:

- Focus on the Speaker

True listening begins with your full attention. Eliminate distractions, make eye contact, and signal through your body language that you're engaged. By being physically present, you show respect and create an environment where the speaker feels valued. Your attention isn't just about hearing—it's about showing that you're fully invested in understanding what's being shared.

- Practice Empathy

Listening with empathy means going beyond the words to understand the speaker's emotions, perspective, and motivations. Instead of forming judgments or planning your response, focus entirely on their experience. For example, if a team member expresses frustration about a challenge, validate their feelings: "I can see how this situation might feel overwhelming. Let's work through it together." Empathy builds connection, making it easier to respond with understanding and support.

- Clarify and Summarize

To ensure accurate understanding, reflect back on what you've heard. Summarize key points, ask clarifying questions, and confirm that your interpretation aligns with their intent. For instance, you might say: "What I'm hearing is that the timeline feels tight and you're concerned about meeting expectations. Is that correct?" This not only prevents miscommunication but also shows the speaker that you're truly committed to capturing their message.

Active listening is transformative. It shifts communication from a transactional exchange to a relational connection. When team members feel heard, they're more likely to trust you, collaborate openly, and contribute their best efforts. They see that their voices matter, which fosters motivation, loyalty, and a shared sense of purpose.

As a leader, your ability to actively listen unlocks the potential of your team. It builds an environment where ideas flow freely, challenges are tackled collaboratively, and misunderstandings are minimized. Most importantly, it creates a foundation of trust and respect that strengthens the entire team.

In a world filled with distractions, active listening is a rare and powerful gift. It requires focus, empathy, and intentionality—but the rewards are profound. By mastering the art of listening, you not only enhance your communication but also create a culture where people feel valued, understood, and inspired to give their best.

Great leaders listen not just to respond but to understand. By embracing active listening, you show your team that leadership isn't about having all the answers—it's about fostering a space where the best answers emerge together.

Active listening starts with cultivating an environment where team members feel safe to express themselves openly. When people fear judgment or dismissal, they're less likely to share their honest thoughts, limiting the team's ability to innovate, solve problems, and grow. As a leader, you set the tone for communication. By being open, nonjudgmental, and receptive, you create a culture where everyone feels encouraged to speak up—whether they're sharing ideas, voicing concerns, or asking for help.

For example, if a team member is struggling with a project, resist the urge to interrupt or immediately jump in with solutions. Allow them to fully express their frustrations or challenges before responding. Show patience and understanding by listening attentively, then offering support or guidance. This reassures your team that they can approach you without fear of judgment or reprimand, building trust and fostering a sense of psychological safety. When people feel safe to communicate openly, they're more willing to engage, collaborate, and contribute their best.

Listening effectively requires more than just hearing words—it involves observing and interpreting nonverbal cues such as body language, tone of voice, and facial expressions. These subtle signals often reveal emotions and intentions that words alone may not convey. By being attuned to these cues, you gain a deeper understanding of your team's experiences, allowing you to respond with empathy and insight.

For instance, if a team member says they're on board with a plan but appears hesitant or withdrawn, take note of this inconsistency. It might indicate unspoken reservations or concerns. Approach them with open-ended questions like, *"I sense there might be more on your mind—would you like to share your thoughts?"* This demonstrates that you value their perspective and are genuinely interested in understanding their feelings.

Empathy lies at the heart of active listening. It doesn't require you to agree with everything being said, but it does mean acknowledging the speaker's emotions and validating their experience. For example, saying, *"I can see why this situation feels overwhelming; let's explore how we can tackle it together,"* shows that you care about their challenges and are invested in their success. Empathetic listening strengthens team morale by fostering a sense of inclusion, understanding, and support.

Clarifying questions are an essential tool for active listening. They ensure that you fully understand what's being communicated while showing the speaker that their words matter. These questions also invite deeper exploration, encouraging the speaker to expand on their thoughts and share additional insights.

For example, if a team member shares a concern about a project timeline, you might ask, *"Can you help me understand what specific challenges you're facing with this deadline?"* This approach not only provides clarity but also signals your genuine interest in finding a solution together.

When asking clarifying questions, aim for open-ended prompts that encourage dialogue rather than yes-or-no answers. Questions like, *"What do you think might help in this situation?"* or *"Can you walk me through your thought process?"* invite reflection and collaboration, strengthening the connection between leader and team.

Creating a safe space for dialogue, practicing empathy, and asking clarifying questions are the building blocks of active listening. These practices foster trust, deepen understanding, and promote a culture of openness where everyone feels valued.

As a leader, your ability to listen effectively transforms

communication into a powerful tool for connection and collaboration. By showing your team that their voices matter, you inspire them to share authentically, engage fully, and work together toward shared goals.

Active listening isn't just about hearing what's said—it's about creating a space where people feel heard, supported, and empowered to succeed.

An essential component of active listening is summarizing or reflecting on what you've heard. This practice accomplishes two key objectives: it confirms your understanding of the speaker's message, and it demonstrates that you value their input enough to ensure accuracy. Reflecting back isn't about parroting their words—it's about capturing the essence of their message in a way that validates their perspective.

For instance, after a team member expresses a concern, you might respond: *"It sounds like you're feeling overwhelmed by the current deadlines and are concerned about meeting expectations. Did I get that right?"* This reflection provides the speaker with an opportunity to confirm, clarify, or expand on their thoughts. It ensures that both of you are aligned and helps avoid potential miscommunications.

This approach is particularly valuable in emotionally charged situations where tensions might otherwise lead to misunderstanding. Taking the time to reflect back shows a level of care and attentiveness that can defuse conflicts and reinforce trust. By seeking confirmation, you demonstrate that their concerns are heard and understood, fostering a stronger connection between you and your team.

Active listening requires patience—a skill that often runs counter to the fast-paced nature of leadership. As a leader, it's natural to want to jump in with solutions or advice, especially when you think you know where the conversation is headed. However, interrupting can disrupt the speaker's thought process and unintentionally convey that you value efficiency over their perspective.

Instead, allow them to finish speaking before you respond, even if you believe you already understand their point. This patience shows respect for their voice and allows them to fully articulate their thoughts. Often, the most important part of someone's message emerges at the end, once they've had time to process and express themselves fully.

Avoiding interruptions also ensures that you're capturing the full context of their message. When you allow the conversation to unfold naturally, your response becomes more thoughtful and informed. This practice doesn't just enhance communication—it models a leadership style that values openness, respect, and collaboration.

For example, during a discussion about workload challenges, resist the urge to immediately suggest solutions. Instead, let the speaker fully explain their perspective, and then reflect: *"I appreciate you sharing this. Let's explore together how we can tackle these challenges effectively."* This approach reinforces that their input is valued and ensures that your response addresses the full scope of their concerns.

Summarizing and reflecting back, coupled with patience and attentiveness, transforms listening from a passive act into a powerful leadership tool. These practices not only ensure clarity but also foster a sense of respect and validation that strengthens trust within your team.

When you take the time to truly listen—without interruptions or assumptions—you create an environment where people feel valued and safe to share their ideas, concerns, and challenges. This culture of open communication paves the way for better collaboration, more innovative problem-solving, and deeper connections between leader and team.

Active listening isn't just about hearing—it's about making people feel heard. And in doing so, you reinforce the bonds of trust and respect that form the foundation of a thriving, resilient team.

Active listening is more than a communication tool—it's a cornerstone of team culture. When leaders listen actively, it creates a ripple effect that shapes how team members engage, collaborate, and support one another. By listening with intention, empathy, and respect, you send a powerful message: Every voice matters. This not only motivates individuals to contribute but also fosters a sense of belonging and purpose within the team.

When team members feel heard and valued, they're more likely to engage fully and authentically. Over time, this practice strengthens trust and builds an environment of open communication. It sets the standard for how people interact—not just with you as the leader, but with each other. Active listening becomes a cultural norm, encouraging team members to approach one another with the same level of respect and empathy.

The benefits of active listening extend far beyond individual conversations. It enhances collaboration by creating a space where ideas flow freely, ensuring everyone feels empowered to contribute. When people know their perspectives will be heard and respected, they're more likely to share creative solutions and participate actively in problem-solving.

Active listening also reduces conflict. Many workplace tensions arise from misunderstandings or unacknowledged concerns. By fostering a culture where people feel safe to express themselves openly, you address issues before they escalate. Listening with empathy and clarity helps diffuse potential conflicts and reinforces a team dynamic built on trust and understanding.

At its core, active listening is about creating a culture where everyone feels valued and respected. This cultural foundation drives better decision-making, as diverse perspectives are considered and integrated. It also cultivates a sense of ownership and accountability, as team members see their contributions reflected in the team's outcomes.

As a leader, prioritizing active listening sets the stage for a cohesive, high-performing team. It shows that leadership isn't just about giving direction—it's about creating the conditions for everyone to thrive. When you listen actively, you don't just hear your team—you empower them.

Active listening isn't just a skill; it's a commitment to fostering connection, trust, and collaboration. Its impact reaches far beyond individual interactions, shaping the very culture of your team. By setting the standard for open, respectful communication, you create an environment where everyone feels heard and valued.

This culture of listening becomes a foundation for growth, resilience, and shared success. It transforms teams into communities of support and innovation, where each member feels empowered to bring their best. And it all starts with one simple yet powerful act: truly listening.

Mastering Clarity and conciseness

In leadership, clarity and conciseness are not just communication skills—they are tools for building trust, driving focus, and ensuring efficiency. When a leader communicates with precision, it prevents misunderstandings, reduces frustration, and empowers the team to stay aligned with their objectives. Clear communication delivers messages that are easy to understand and actionable. Conciseness ensures those messages are focused, free of unnecessary details that might obscure the core idea. Together, these qualities foster a more productive and cohesive team environment.

Your team relies on you for guidance, direction, and focus.

Clear communication provides them with confidence—they know what's expected, why it matters, and how to move forward. On the other hand, vague or overly complex messages can lead to confusion, delays, and even mistakes. Mastering clarity and conciseness not only gives your team the tools they need to succeed but also strengthens your credibility as a leader.

The key to clear and concise communication is defining your purpose before you speak. Ask yourself:

- *What is the main point I need to communicate?*
- *What action do I want my team to take after hearing this?*

By clarifying your purpose, you can focus on the core message and eliminate distractions. This intentionality ensures your communication is streamlined and impactful, increasing the likelihood that your team will understand and act on it.

For instance, if you're providing feedback on a project, be specific about your goal. Are you recognizing achievements? Highlighting areas for improvement? Setting expectations for future tasks? When your purpose is clear, your message becomes more focused, avoiding mixed signals and ensuring your team knows exactly what to do next.

To communicate with clarity, prioritize simplicity. Avoid jargon or overly complex language that might confuse your audience. Break down your message into key points, ensuring each one is essential and directly tied to your purpose.

For example, instead of saying:

"We need to focus on improving operational efficiencies to enhance overall outcomes and streamline outputs."

Try:

"Let's focus on making our process faster and more efficient. This will help us deliver better results with less effort."

This approach simplifies the message, making it easier for your team to understand and act upon.

Conciseness is about saying enough to inform, but not so much that the message becomes diluted. Be intentional with your words, ensuring each one adds value to the communication. If a detail doesn't serve the main purpose, consider whether it's necessary to include.

For example, when giving instructions, avoid lengthy explanations that may confuse rather than clarify. Instead of:

"We have to prioritize Task A because it impacts Task B, which is connected to the client's expectations, and we want to ensure no delays for the deliverables."

Say:

"Let's prioritize Task A to meet the client's deadline."

This approach saves time, reduces misunderstandings, and ensures the focus remains on what matters most.

Mastering clarity and conciseness strengthens team culture by creating a foundation of trust and efficiency. When your team knows they can rely on you for clear, actionable guidance, they feel more confident in their work and more connected to the team's goals. This practice reduces frustration, increases productivity, and fosters a collaborative environment where everyone understands their role and purpose.

By defining your purpose, simplifying your message, and eliminating unnecessary details, you set a standard for communication that inspires confidence and drives results. Leadership isn't just about what you say—it's about how effectively you say it.

As a leader, it's tempting to use industry-specific jargon or technical terms, especially when they're second nature to you. However, not everyone on your team may be as familiar with these terms, and using them can unintentionally create confusion or alienation. Effective leaders simplify their language, ensuring their messages are accessible and relatable to everyone.

Before communicating, consider your audience's familiarity

with the topic. Ask yourself: Will everyone understand this term? Could it be misinterpreted? When in doubt, opt for straightforward, unambiguous language. If technical terms are necessary, take a moment to explain them in simple terms.

For example, instead of saying, *"We need to align stakeholders to ensure buy-in on this cross-functional integration,"* try, *"We need everyone's support to make sure this project runs smoothly across departments."* By replacing jargon with everyday language, you make your message more relatable and reduce potential misunderstandings.

Analogies or simplified explanations can also be powerful tools. For instance, if you're describing a technical process, relate it to something familiar: *"Think of this system like a relay race—each phase depends on the smooth handoff from the one before it."* These strategies ensure that your message resonates with your audience, fostering clarity and connection.

Leadership often involves communicating multifaceted or technical concepts. When presenting complex information, breaking it down into manageable parts helps your team follow along without feeling overwhelmed.

Start by identifying the most critical points. Ask yourself: What does my team absolutely need to know right now? Present these points in a logical sequence, focusing on clarity and simplicity. For example, when introducing a new project, begin with the big picture—its overall objective. Then, break it into phases, outlining the specific goals, timelines, and dependencies of each.

This step-by-step approach prevents information overload, giving team members a clear understanding of how each part fits into the whole. For example:

1. Objective: Define the purpose of the project.

2. Phases: Outline key stages and milestones.

    3.   Timelines: Share deadlines for each phase.

    4.   Responsibilities: Highlight roles and expectations.

Using visual aids like charts, diagrams, or bullet points can further simplify complex information. Visuals provide a quick summary and help clarify relationships between concepts, making it easier for your team to process and retain the information. For instance, a Gantt chart can illustrate timelines and dependencies at a glance, while a flowchart can map out processes step by step.

By presenting information in digestible portions and leveraging visuals where appropriate, you set your team up for success. You minimize confusion, build confidence, and ensure everyone feels equipped to tackle even the most complex challenges.

Avoiding jargon and breaking down complex information are essential skills for effective leadership communication. When you simplify your language and structure your message thoughtfully, you create a shared understanding that aligns your team and drives action.

Leadership isn't about demonstrating how much you know— it's about ensuring your team understands and feels confident in what they're doing. By focusing on clarity, relatability, and accessibility, you foster a culture of collaboration and trust, empowering your team to perform at their best.

In leadership, clarity is not just about delivering information; it's about spotlighting what matters most. When communicating with your team, emphasize key points or priorities to ensure they stand out. This focus helps your team understand where to direct their energy and prevents critical details from getting lost in the shuffle of less important information.

If your message involves multiple details, clearly identify which ones require immediate attention. For example, if you're assigning a project with several tasks, highlight the high-priority items:

"The most important part of this project is completing the initial research phase by Friday. Once we have that information, we can move forward with the other tasks."

By explicitly stating priorities, you enable your team to manage their workload effectively, reducing stress and improving overall productivity.

Reinforcing key points at the end of a conversation or summarizing them in writing can also enhance clarity. A brief recap ensures everyone leaves with a clear understanding of expectations. For instance: *"To summarize, the top priority is completing the research phase by Friday. Let me know if you run into any challenges."*

Even the clearest communication can occasionally be misunderstood. To ensure your message lands as intended, actively seek feedback from your team. Encourage them to ask questions or repeat back their understanding of the instructions. This creates a feedback loop that allows you to address any potential misunderstandings before they escalate into problems.

For instance, after explaining a task, you could say: *"Can you walk me through how you plan to tackle this? I want to make sure I've explained it clearly."* This approach not only confirms their understanding but also provides an opportunity for team members to voice any uncertainties.

Encouraging questions signals that you're approachable and committed to effective communication. When team members know they can seek clarity without judgment, it fosters a culture of openness and mutual respect.

Regularly asking for feedback also improves your communication skills by giving you insights into how your messages are received. This iterative process helps you refine your approach and ensures consistent alignment between you and your team.

In a fast-paced environment, brevity is invaluable. Speaking only as much as needed to convey your message saves time, reduces confusion, and keeps your team focused. Brevity doesn't mean omitting essential details; rather, it's about eliminating unnecessary ones that might dilute the main point.

Before communicating, ask yourself:

- Is this detail necessary?
- Does it add value to the message?

This habit of filtering extraneous information sharpens your communication and shows respect for your team's time and attention. For example, instead of saying:

"We need to enhance efficiency by addressing bottlenecks in our process to ensure smoother handoffs between teams and ultimately improve our overall productivity,"

Try:

"Let's address the bottlenecks to improve team efficiency and productivity."

In written communication, brevity is equally important. Long emails or dense messages risk being skimmed, leading to missed details. Use bullet points, short paragraphs, or headers to make key points stand out. For example:

- Priority 1: Complete the research phase by Friday.
- Priority 2: Begin the initial draft after the research is reviewed.
- Resources: Reach out to [Name] for data support.

This approach makes your message clear, actionable, and easy to follow.

Mastering clarity and conciseness is an ongoing practice, but its impact on your leadership is transformative. By emphasizing key points, seeking feedback, and practicing brevity, you create an environment where your team feels confident and focused.

When your team knows exactly what's expected of them, they're empowered to perform at their best. Clear, concise communication ensures they have the information they need to succeed, reducing stress and enhancing collaboration. In leadership, your words are not just instructions—they're a tool to inspire and guide your team toward shared goals.

Navigating Difficult Conversations

As a leader, navigating difficult conversations is part of the job—a responsibility that can be both uncomfortable and transformative. These are the moments when leadership truly matters: addressing performance issues, providing constructive feedback, resolving conflicts, or tackling uncomfortable topics. While these conversations may feel daunting, they're opportunities to strengthen relationships, build trust, and guide your team toward growth.

Handled well, difficult conversations demonstrate your commitment to openness, respect, and continuous improvement. They show your team that you care enough to address challenges directly, rather than avoiding them. By approaching these discussions with empathy, clarity, and a focus on positive outcomes, you create an environment where people feel supported and motivated to grow.

Preparation is essential for making difficult conversations productive and respectful. Before diving in, take time to clarify your purpose and goals. Ask yourself:

- What do I hope to achieve from this conversation?
- What specific issues need to be addressed?
- How can I frame this discussion constructively?

Having a clear sense of your objectives helps you stay focused, calm, and intentional. It also prevents the conversation from veering into unproductive territory.

Anticipate the other person's perspective and potential reactions. Consider how they might feel hearing this feedback and prepare responses that acknowledge their emotions. This doesn't mean predicting exactly what they'll say but being ready to approach the conversation with empathy and understanding.

For example, if you're addressing a performance issue, gather specific examples to illustrate your concerns. Avoid vague statements like, "You need to improve your work ethic." Instead, use concrete observations: "I've noticed that deadlines have been missed on three recent projects, and I'd like to understand what's happening so we can find a solution together." This approach shifts the focus from blame to collaboration, setting a constructive tone from the start.

Approaching difficult conversations with empathy helps create a supportive and constructive environment. Start by recognizing that the conversation may feel uncomfortable or stressful for the other person. Use active listening to show that you value their perspective, allowing them to express their thoughts and feelings without interruption. This approach fosters mutual respect and encourages open dialogue.

For example, if a team member is struggling to meet expectations, begin by acknowledging their efforts and the challenges they may be facing. Then, provide space for them to share their perspective. Listen attentively, and ask clarifying questions if needed to fully understand their experience. An empathy-driven approach reduces defensiveness and promotes collaborative problem-solving.

By listening actively, you demonstrate that your focus extends beyond the immediate outcome to include their well-being and professional growth. This creates an atmosphere of trust, where team members feel more comfortable engaging in difficult conversations, knowing they will be met with understanding rather than judgment.

In challenging conversations, it's essential to focus on the issue at hand rather than making it personal. Address specific behaviors, actions, or outcomes instead of criticizing the individual. This approach reduces defensiveness and encourages the person to focus on improvement rather than feeling attacked.

For instance, instead of saying, *"You're not committed enough to your work,"* reframe the issue as, *"I've noticed that deadlines have been missed more frequently lately, and I'd like to discuss ways we can ensure projects stay on track."* By addressing the behavior rather than the person, you create a more objective and constructive atmosphere where improvement feels achievable.

Keeping the conversation centered on the issue also prevents unproductive arguments or emotional reactions. When the discussion focuses on solutions rather than blame, it's easier to work together toward outcomes that benefit both the individual and the team.

When addressing sensitive topics, it's natural to want to soften your message to avoid discomfort. But clear and direct language is critical for effective communication, especially during difficult conversations. Being direct doesn't mean being harsh—it means delivering your message in a way that leaves no room for misinterpretation while maintaining respect.

For example, if you need to address a performance issue, avoid ambiguous statements like, *"Things could be better."* Instead, be specific and direct: *"I've noticed that the last two reports were submitted late, and I'd like to discuss how we can ensure deadlines are consistently met moving forward."* This approach ensures the individual understands what needs to change and why, while framing the conversation as a path toward improvement.

Clear communication eliminates confusion and sets a positive tone for action. When people know exactly what's expected, they're better equipped to make meaningful changes. By combining directness with empathy, you can ensure your message is clear while maintaining trust and respect.

One of the most effective ways to navigate a difficult conversation is by collaborating on solutions. When you involve team members in finding answers, it fosters a sense of ownership and engagement, empowering them to take an active role in addressing the issue. Instead of prescribing fixes, ask questions that invite their input. This collaborative approach reinforces that the conversation is about growth, not criticism.

For example, after discussing a performance issue, you might ask, *"What steps do you think could help address this challenge?"* or *"How can I support you in meeting these expectations?"* These questions show that you're not only invested in the outcome but also in their success. It communicates that you're willing to work together and respect their autonomy, making the conversation a partnership rather than a directive.

Ending the conversation with a clear action plan is essential. Summarize the key points discussed, outline any support or resources you'll provide, and agree on a timeline for follow-up. For instance, you could say, *"To recap, we've identified [specific steps], and I'll check in with you in two weeks to see how things are progressing."*

This final step ensures that both of you leave the conversation aligned, with shared clarity about what's next. It transforms what could feel like criticism into an opportunity for growth, leaving the individual empowered and motivated to move forward.

Following up after a difficult conversation is essential for reinforcing progress and maintaining trust. Checking in with team members shows that you're committed to their growth beyond the initial discussion and that you genuinely care about their development. It also provides an opportunity to address any ongoing challenges and celebrate improvements.

For example, if the conversation involved setting new performance goals, schedule a follow-up meeting a few weeks later to review progress. Use this time to discuss what's going well, acknowledge positive changes, and offer constructive feedback on areas that still need attention. This check-in keeps the lines of communication open and helps them stay on track toward their goals.

Consistent follow-up also demonstrates accountability. When leaders take the time to follow through, it reinforces the idea that the conversation wasn't just a one-time event—it's part of a long-term commitment to growth. Team members feel supported and valued, which turns what could have been a difficult experience into an opportunity for ongoing improvement. This approach not only strengthens the individual but also helps build a more cohesive and resilient team.

Leveraging Nonverbal Communication

Nonverbal communication is one of the most powerful tools in leadership, often conveying as much—if not more—than spoken words. While it's easy to focus on what we say, how we say it—through body language, facial expressions, and tone—can profoundly impact how our message is received. Nonverbal cues can either reinforce our words or contradict them, influencing how others perceive our confidence, approachability, and sincerity. For leaders, mastering nonverbal communication strengthens connection, builds trust, and ensures that messages are delivered with clarity and credibility.

Effectively leveraging nonverbal communication requires self-awareness and intention. Leaders who are mindful of their nonverbal cues can create a strong impression, fostering an environment of respect, openness, and collaboration. By aligning verbal and nonverbal communication, you enhance the impact of your message, creating a cohesive and engaging way to interact with your team.

Body language—our gestures, posture, and movements—reveals emotions, attitudes, and intentions, often unconsciously. Positive, open body language signals approachability and attentiveness, while closed or tense body language can create barriers. Being mindful of your body language as a leader helps convey confidence and openness, making team members feel at ease communicating with you.

For example, standing or sitting with an open posture—relaxed shoulders, uncrossed arms, and facing the person directly—demonstrates attentiveness and receptiveness. Leaning slightly forward during a conversation shows interest, while maintaining a balanced, upright posture communicates confidence. Avoid crossing your arms, which can come across as defensive or unapproachable, especially during sensitive discussions.

In group settings, your physical positioning matters. Ensure you're visible to everyone and move naturally to engage different parts of the room. This inclusive body language shows that you're addressing everyone, reinforcing unity and respect within the team.

Eye contact is one of the most impactful forms of nonverbal communication, creating a direct connection between you and your listener. When used effectively, eye contact conveys confidence, sincerity, and attentiveness, signaling that you're engaged and genuinely interested in the conversation. This builds trust and rapport, while a lack of eye contact can come across as disengaged, evasive, or untrustworthy.

When speaking one-on-one, maintain consistent eye contact to show you're fully present, but avoid staring, which can feel uncomfortable or intimidating. Aim for a natural rhythm, occasionally breaking eye contact to allow the conversation to flow comfortably.

In group settings, share your eye contact with everyone, moving your gaze around the room to include each individual.

This practice reinforces that everyone is an integral part of the discussion and makes them feel acknowledged. Eye contact is particularly impactful when delivering key points, as it underscores the importance of your message and reinforces your confidence as a leader.

Facial expressions are a direct reflection of our emotions and play a crucial role in nonverbal communication. A smile, a nod, or an empathetic expression can show that you're engaged, approachable, and understanding. When your facial expressions align with your message, they reinforce your words, creating authenticity that resonates with your team.

For example, when delivering positive feedback, a genuine smile and nod emphasize that you're truly pleased with their performance, making your appreciation more impactful. During serious conversations, a neutral or empathetic expression shows that you're taking the matter seriously, reassuring the team member that you understand the significance of the issue.

Be mindful of unconscious expressions that might unintentionally undermine your message. For instance, furrowing your brows or frowning during a team member's presentation might be interpreted as disapproval, even if you're simply deep in thought. Practicing self-awareness and ensuring your expressions match your intentions conveys respect, attentiveness, and empathy.

Your tone of voice—the pitch, volume, and inflection—has a profound impact on how your message is received. A calm, steady tone communicates confidence and authority, while a softer tone conveys empathy and approachability. Conversely, a high or overly loud tone can come across as anxious or confrontational, potentially putting the listener on edge.

When delivering instructions or guidance, a confident and even tone reassures your team. In sensitive discussions, a gentler tone fosters a safe space for open dialogue. Adjusting your tone based on the situation allows you to communicate effectively while respecting the emotional context of the conversation.

Pacing also plays a critical role. Speaking too quickly may signal nervousness or impatience, while speaking too slowly can seem condescending. A natural, moderate pace encourages attentiveness, giving your listener time to process the information. By being mindful of your tone and pacing, you ensure your message aligns with your intentions and fosters a positive interaction.

Nonverbal communication isn't just about expressing yourself—it's also about interpreting the cues of others. Observing your team members' body language, facial expressions, and tone of voice can provide valuable insights into their emotions, engagement levels, and reactions to your message. Recognizing these cues allows you to adapt your approach, creating a more empathetic and responsive communication style.

For example, if a team member crosses their arms or avoids eye contact, it might indicate discomfort, disengagement, or disagreement. Use this observation as an opportunity to ask open-ended questions or invite them to share their thoughts, creating space to address their concerns. Similarly, if someone leans in and nods frequently, it signals engagement and receptiveness, reinforcing that your message is resonating positively.

Responding to nonverbal cues demonstrates attentiveness and adaptability, qualities that enhance your credibility as a leader. By staying aware of how your team members are reacting, you create dynamic interactions that build trust and encourage open communication.

For nonverbal communication to be effective, it must align with your verbal message. When your words and nonverbal cues are in harmony, they create a sense of authenticity and reinforce your message. However, a mismatch—such as using positive words with a disengaged tone or expression—can make your message seem insincere, leading to confusion or mistrust.

For instance, if you offer praise but appear distracted or neutral, the recipient may doubt the genuineness of your compliment. Conversely, delivering constructive feedback with a warm, empathetic tone shows that you're supportive and invested in their improvement. Aligning verbal and nonverbal cues ensures your message is clear, credible, and respectful, making it easier for your team to trust and respond to you.

Consistency between your words and body language is particularly critical during high-stakes conversations, where trust and clarity are paramount. When your verbal and nonverbal communication align, you project authenticity and demonstrate self-awareness, both of which resonate positively with your team.

Mastering nonverbal communication enhances your ability to lead with empathy and impact. When your body language, facial expressions, and tone complement your words, you create a cohesive and powerful message. This alignment not only engages your team but also fosters a deeper sense of trust and respect. Nonverbal communication adds depth to your leadership style, making your interactions more meaningful and effective.

Making Decisions with Confidence

Understanding the Weight of Leadership Decisions

One of the defining responsibilities of leadership is decision-making. Every choice a leader makes, whether big or small, carries weight because it affects more than just tasks and processes—it impacts people's motivation, trust, and productivity. As a new leader, it's crucial to recognize that your decisions have far-reaching implications beyond immediate outcomes. The ability to make choices confidently and thoughtfully is a cornerstone of effective leadership, requiring self-awareness and a deep understanding of your team's needs and goals.

Unlike individual contributors, who focus primarily on optimizing their tasks, leaders must consider how each decision aligns with broader objectives, impacts team dynamics, and reflects their values. Leadership decision-making is about foresight and responsibility, not just action. It involves weighing potential outcomes, managing risks, and anticipating the ripple effects on the team, the project, and the organization as a whole.

A critical aspect of leadership decision-making is balancing short-term needs with long-term goals. While some decisions offer immediate solutions, they can have unintended consequences if not carefully considered. As a leader, it's essential to recognize when a quick fix might compromise future objectives, team morale, or the quality of outcomes. Conversely, delaying decisions or being overly cautious can lead to inefficiencies, missed opportunities, and frustration within the team.

For instance, if your team faces a tight deadline, a short-term solution might involve redistributing workloads or asking for overtime. While this could resolve the immediate issue, it might also lead to burnout, resentment, or declining work quality. Alternatively, a more sustainable approach might involve reassessing resource allocation, setting realistic deadlines, or providing additional support to prevent similar challenges in the future.

Effective leaders weigh the present and future impacts of their choices, striving for a balance between immediate needs and strategic goals. This approach not only strengthens decision-making but also reassures your team that you are invested in their long-term success and well-being.

Leadership decisions directly affect team trust and morale. Arbitrary or inconsistent choices can create uncertainty, eroding trust and engagement. In contrast, thoughtful, transparent decisions that align with team values and goals build trust, cohesion, and motivation. As a leader, it's important to consider how your decisions will be perceived by your team, as this perception influences their confidence in your leadership.

Before deciding, ask yourself: *How will this affect the team's trust in my judgment? Will it feel fair? Does it align with the values I've communicated?* For example, if transparency is one of your core values, explain the rationale behind difficult or unexpected decisions. Even when a choice isn't popular, being open about your thought process shows honesty and respect for the team's need for clarity.

Decisions that demonstrate empathy and consideration for the team's experience further boost morale. If a decision results in extra workload, offer additional support or express genuine appreciation for their efforts. When team members feel their contributions and challenges are acknowledged, they're more likely to approach obstacles with resilience and commitment.

High-stakes decisions—such as resolving conflicts, managing project risks, or responding to unexpected changes—can place immense pressure on leaders. These decisions often carry significant consequences for your team's success and well-being, making it critical to approach them thoughtfully. While the weight of these moments can feel intimidating, they also provide an opportunity to demonstrate resilience and model how to handle challenges with composure.

When faced with high-stakes decisions, taking a structured approach can help reduce stress and improve clarity. Break the decision into smaller components, evaluating each factor independently. Identify key risks, potential rewards, and the resources available to support your team. By systematically analyzing the situation, you gain perspective and minimize the risk of reacting impulsively under pressure.

In addition to logical analysis, trust your intuition. Leadership often requires balancing data with gut instinct, especially when navigating unfamiliar territory. Your intuition, shaped by experience, values, and an understanding of your team's needs, offers valuable insights that complement rational evaluation. By integrating instinct with analysis, you can make confident decisions, even in uncertain or high-pressure scenarios.

No leader makes perfect decisions every time. Mistakes are inevitable, particularly when tackling complex challenges. However, each mistake is an opportunity to learn, refine your decision-making skills, and grow as a leader. Embracing mistakes as part of the process allows you to reframe them not as failures, but as feedback that informs your future choices.

After making a decision, take time to reflect on both the outcome and the process. Ask yourself questions such as:

- What went well?
- What could have been done differently?
- How did the team respond?

Reflection helps you assess the impact of your choices and identify areas for improvement. Additionally, seeking feedback from your team provides valuable perspectives on how decisions affect morale, motivation, and performance. This collaborative approach to learning fosters mutual trust and continuous improvement.

By viewing mistakes as stepping stones in your growth, you cultivate a mindset that values resilience and adaptability. When your team sees you embrace setbacks as learning opportunities, they're more likely to adopt the same approach, creating a culture that encourages progress over perfection.

The Role of Data and Intuition

In leadership, decisions are often complex, involving factors that can be difficult to quantify or predict. As a leader, your responsibility is to guide your team by leveraging both available information and your understanding of the broader context. Data and intuition are two powerful tools that can support this process. Data provides objective insights, validating or challenging assumptions, while intuition—your inner sense of what feels right based on experience and judgment—adds a personal, human dimension to decision-making. Effective leaders strike a balance between these two elements, using each to complement and enhance the other.

Some decisions naturally lend themselves to data-driven approaches, while others require an intuitive grasp of team dynamics, values, or organizational culture. By honing your skills in both areas, you can make informed, insightful choices that account for both the tangible and intangible aspects of leadership.

Data offers an invaluable foundation for objective decision-making. It allows leaders to base choices on measurable insights rather than assumptions, reducing bias and increasing the reliability of outcomes. Data can come from many sources, such as performance metrics, survey feedback, financial reports, or industry trends. By analyzing this information, you can identify patterns, assess risks, and seize opportunities, all of which lead to more grounded and precise decisions.

For instance, if you're considering allocating additional resources to a project, data on past performance, current workload distribution, and resource utilization can provide a clearer picture of potential benefits and challenges. When the data aligns with your objectives, it reinforces the credibility of the decision and allows you to communicate it with confidence to your team.

However, data is most effective when it's relevant and focused. Not every metric is useful for every decision. By concentrating on key indicators that align directly with your goals, you can avoid information overload and maintain clarity. Prioritize core data points that inform the decision at hand and use these insights to bolster your reasoning.

While data is a powerful tool, it's not without its limitations. Overreliance on data can result in decisions that overlook important context, team dynamics, or unforeseen variables. Data tells part of the story, but it doesn't capture everything, particularly in areas involving human emotions, relationships, or values. Numbers alone may not reflect morale, motivation, or potential resistance to change within a team.

Additionally, data can be influenced by factors such as sample size, measurement error, or timing. A single data point or trend may not reflect the full reality, especially in a rapidly changing environment. For example, a dip in performance metrics might suggest decreased productivity, but it could also result from temporary external factors, such as a particularly demanding project phase or personal challenges faced by team members.

Recognizing these limitations is essential. Rather than viewing data as the sole source of truth, treat it as one component of a larger decision-making framework. Use data to guide your understanding, but be prepared to consider additional context when necessary. This balanced approach prevents overreliance on numbers and ensures that your decisions account for both objective evidence and the real-world nuances of leadership.

Intuition—the gut feeling that arises from experience, values, and a deep understanding of a situation—is a powerful element of leadership decision-making. While it may lack the objectivity of data, intuition provides an invaluable human perspective, enabling leaders to make insightful, adaptable choices. This is particularly critical in situations where data is limited, inconclusive, or unable to account for complex human dynamics.

Trusting your intuition doesn't mean making impulsive or uninformed decisions. Instead, it involves drawing on past experiences, knowledge of your team, and alignment with your goals to make choices that feel consistent with your values and purpose. For example, if you sense that a particular strategy might not resonate with your team, even when data suggests it's effective, trust that instinct and explore alternative approaches. Intuition often reveals potential issues that data alone might overlook, helping you anticipate challenges before they arise.

Developing intuition takes self-awareness and intentional reflection. Regularly assess past decisions, identifying what worked well and where improvements could be made. These reflections deepen your intuitive understanding and strengthen your ability to make confident, well-rounded decisions.

The most effective leadership decisions come from a balanced approach that integrates data and intuition. Data provides factual insights, while intuition adds the context and perspective needed to interpret those insights effectively. Together, they create a comprehensive foundation for informed, adaptable decision-making.

For instance, imagine deciding whether to implement a new team structure based on data showing inefficiencies. The data may suggest an immediate need for change, but your intuition—grounded in your understanding of team morale and culture—warns that a sudden shift could disrupt cohesion. A balanced approach might involve using data to justify the restructuring while implementing it gradually, respecting team dynamics and allowing time for adjustment.

When data and intuition align, the decision feels stronger, giving you confidence that objective evidence and personal judgment both support your choice. However, when they seem to conflict, take time to explore the discrepancy. Ask yourself why your intuition hesitates and whether additional data might provide clarity. Balancing these elements ensures that your decisions are both thorough and nuanced, accounting for measurable outcomes and your team's well-being.

As you develop your ability to balance data and intuition, reflection becomes a key practice. After each decision, evaluate its outcome and the roles that data and intuition played in the process. Consider questions such as:

- How did the data support or challenge my intuition?
- What insights did my intuition provide that data couldn't capture?

This reflective practice helps refine your approach, teaching you how to better integrate these elements in future decisions.

Gathering feedback from your team can also provide valuable

insights into how your decisions impact them. This feedback helps you assess whether your decision-making approach aligns with their needs and expectations, guiding you in determining when to rely more on data or intuition.

By making reflection a consistent part of your leadership journey, you develop a deeper awareness of how data and intuition intersect. Over time, this practice builds your confidence, adaptability, and decision-making effectiveness, enabling you to make choices that resonate with your team and align with your organization's goals.

In leadership, data and intuition are complementary tools. Data provides structure and objectivity, while intuition offers insight and adaptability. By cultivating skills in both areas and learning to balance them, you enhance your capacity to make thoughtful, confident decisions that support your team's growth, trust, and success.

Involving the Team in Decision-Making

One of the most effective ways to build trust, engagement, and ownership within your team is by involving them in decision-making. Collaborative decision-making isn't about relinquishing authority; it's about creating a culture where everyone feels their input matters, their ideas are valued, and they have a stake in the team's success. Including your team in decisions fosters diverse perspectives, encourages open communication, and strengthens their commitment to shared goals. When team members feel heard, they're more likely to contribute fully, support the decision, and work together with purpose.

As a leader, your role in team decision-making is to guide the process—ensuring that everyone has an opportunity to contribute while maintaining a clear sense of direction. Effective collaboration requires balance: involving the team enough to foster engagement but retaining responsibility for the ultimate outcome. By knowing when and how to involve your team, you build trust, boost morale, and create a cohesive, collaborative dynamic.

Involving the team in decision-making offers several key advantages:

1.   Fresh Perspectives: Each team member brings unique experiences, skills, and insights that can uncover challenges, spark innovative ideas, or highlight overlooked opportunities. Decisions made with diverse input are often more comprehensive and well-rounded, increasing the likelihood of success.

2.   Ownership and Commitment: When team members participate in shaping decisions, they feel a stronger sense of ownership. Even if the final decision isn't their first choice, they're more likely to support it because they were part of the process. This engagement boosts morale, accountability, and motivation, as team members align their efforts with the team's objectives.

3.   Strengthened Trust and Openness: Inviting team members to contribute demonstrates respect for their ideas and shows that their input is valued. This transparency fosters trust, as the team sees you're committed to considering various viewpoints and making decisions that reflect their collective interests.

While team involvement has clear benefits, not every decision requires or benefits from a collaborative approach. Leaders must assess the nature of each decision and decide whether it's best handled individually, collaboratively, or with selective input.

When to Involve the Team:

Decisions that affect the team's work environment,

workflows, or shared goals are excellent candidates for collaboration. For example, adjusting project timelines, reprioritizing tasks, or implementing new policies can benefit from team input. Engaging the team in these scenarios helps gauge potential impacts, uncover valuable insights, and build consensus.

When to Take a Directive Approach:

Some situations call for a more independent decision-making process, such as those involving confidential information, urgent matters, or highly specialized issues. In these cases, it's essential to communicate the decision transparently. Explain the rationale behind the choice, emphasizing the need for a swift or private approach. Clarifying why team input wasn't sought maintains trust by showing that transparency remains a priority.

By thoughtfully involving your team in decision-making, you empower them to contribute, collaborate, and align with the shared mission. This approach not only enhances the quality of decisions but also strengthens trust and engagement, building a resilient team culture that thrives on openness and mutual respect.

When involving your team in a decision, establish a clear process that fosters open dialogue, respects diverse perspectives, and drives toward a constructive outcome. Start by framing the decision: explain the issue at hand, provide relevant context, and outline the goals and constraints. This clarity helps your team understand the decision's scope and align their input with the objectives.

Encourage each team member to share their perspective, creating an environment where all voices are valued. Use open-ended questions to guide the discussion, such as, "What challenges do you foresee with this approach?" or "What solutions would you recommend to achieve our goals?" These types of questions invite thoughtful contributions and demonstrate that their insights are both needed and appreciated.

As the conversation progresses, facilitate a discussion that explores common themes, compares ideas, and identifies potential solutions. Summarize key points periodically to ensure alignment and address any ambiguities. This structured approach keeps the discussion focused and productive, preventing it from straying off course.

Once all input has been gathered, clarify how the final decision will be made. In some cases, the team may reach a consensus. In others, you might synthesize their input and make the decision yourself. Be transparent about your role, explaining whether their input will directly shape the outcome or serve as guidance for your final choice.

Collaborative decision-making doesn't mean relinquishing your leadership role. Striking a balance between team involvement and your authority is essential for an effective process. As a leader, your responsibility is to guide the discussion, encourage constructive participation, and keep the team focused on the decision's goals. By framing the conversation and setting clear expectations, you create a collaborative environment that values team input while upholding your leadership.

For example, if the decision ultimately rests with you, communicate this openly. You might say, *"I want to hear everyone's thoughts on this issue before making a final decision. Your perspectives will help shape the best course of action."* This approach clarifies your role while reinforcing that their contributions are essential to the process.

Balancing authority with collaboration shows your team that you value their input without compromising your responsibility as a leader. This balance fosters trust, as team members see you as both approachable and decisive.

After a collaborative decision is made, seek feedback on the process and outcome. This feedback demonstrates your commitment to continuous improvement and helps refine future decision-making. Ask questions like, "How did you feel about the decision-making process?" or "What could we do differently next time to make this process more effective?" These questions encourage honest feedback, enabling you to adjust your approach based on the team's needs and experiences.

Evaluating the decision's outcome also reinforces accountability. If the decision leads to success, celebrate the team's role in making it happen. Acknowledging achievements that result from collaboration strengthens the value of teamwork and inspires continued participation.

If the decision doesn't produce the desired results, treat it as an opportunity to learn. Discuss what went well, what could have been improved, and how the process might be refined moving forward. By approaching challenges as learning experiences, you foster a growth-oriented culture where team members feel empowered to contribute without fear of failure.

Collaborative decision-making strengthens team morale, trust, and commitment. When team members see that their contributions are valued and respected, they become more engaged and invested in the outcomes. By balancing team involvement with your leadership role, you create a cohesive, resilient team culture built on mutual respect and shared purpose. This approach not only improves decision-making but also inspires your team to work together with enthusiasm and confidence.

Decision-Making in Times of Uncertainty

Uncertainty is an inevitable part of leadership. Whether it's navigating rapidly changing market conditions, incomplete information, or unforeseen challenges, leaders often face decisions without a clear view of the outcome. In these moments, decision-making can feel overwhelming, as every choice carries the potential for both risk and reward. Yet, uncertainty also presents an opportunity—a chance to demonstrate resilience, adaptability, and the ability to lead with confidence despite ambiguity.

Making decisions under uncertainty requires a thoughtful, flexible approach. While you may not have all the answers, you can guide your team by focusing on what you do know, staying open to adjustments, and leading with transparency. By embracing uncertainty as a natural aspect of leadership, you establish trust and stability, helping your team remain focused, adaptable, and motivated even in challenging times.

In uncertain situations, anchoring your decisions in core objectives and values provides stability and clarity. When information is limited, return to the overarching goals of your team or organization. Ask yourself, *What outcome aligns best with our mission, values, and long-term vision?* This focus grounds your decisions in purpose, even when external factors are unclear.

For example, if your team is faced with a sudden shift in project priorities due to external changes, revisiting your core objectives can clarify what matters most. Perhaps it's maintaining customer satisfaction, upholding quality standards, or meeting key performance goals. By aligning your decisions with these values, you reinforce a sense of consistency and direction, reassuring your team that their work remains guided by clear and meaningful principles.

Anchoring decisions in values not only provides clarity but also boosts team morale. When people see that choices align with shared values, they feel a sense of purpose and unity. This shared focus helps the team stay resilient and motivated, even in the face of uncertainty.

Uncertainty can create a sense of overwhelm, especially when decisions feel complex or high-stakes. Breaking decisions into manageable steps makes the process more approachable, allowing you to focus on one aspect at a time. This incremental approach reduces stress, sharpens focus, and helps you make progress even when the larger picture remains unclear.

For instance, if you're considering a pivot in project strategy, begin by isolating the specific areas that require adjustment. The first step might involve gathering input from team members or assessing the feasibility of alternative approaches. By addressing one component of the decision at a time, you gain clarity and build momentum without needing to solve the entire challenge upfront.

This step-by-step process also fosters flexibility. As you complete each stage, you can reassess the situation, adapt to new information, and refine your approach. In uncertain environments, this adaptability is essential—it ensures that your team remains responsive and poised to tackle evolving challenges, rather than being constrained by a rigid plan.

Uncertainty demands a flexible mindset and a readiness to adapt. Instead of committing fully to one course of action, consider crafting a primary plan supported by backup options. Contingency planning allows you to anticipate challenges and pivot quickly when circumstances shift. This proactive approach not only strengthens your ability to lead decisively but also minimizes the risks inherent in unpredictable situations.

When developing a plan, think through potential "what-if" scenarios. Ask yourself, *What will we do if the situation changes unexpectedly? How will we adapt if certain resources become unavailable?* Preparing for alternative outcomes fosters a sense of control and assurance, even in the face of uncertainty.

Sharing these contingency plans with your team builds trust. When they see that you've thought through different possibilities, they feel reassured that you're prepared to handle unforeseen challenges. This confidence allows them to focus on their work rather than worry about potential disruptions, creating a more stable and productive environment.

Uncertainty is best navigated with diverse perspectives, as varied viewpoints can uncover insights that might otherwise be missed. Involve your team in the decision-making process, inviting them to share their ideas, concerns, and suggestions. A collaborative approach broadens your understanding and helps identify potential solutions or risks that a single perspective might overlook.

When seeking input, be upfront about the complexities involved. Let your team know that while the situation may be challenging, their insights are valuable and appreciated. Encourage brainstorming and constructive discussions where everyone feels safe to share without fear of judgment. This openness fosters a sense of collective responsibility, as the team works together to navigate the uncertainty.

For example, if shifting market conditions are affecting your project, involve the team in exploring possible adjustments. Ask questions like, *How would you approach this challenge? What factors should we prioritize? Do you have suggestions for adapting our plan?* This shared approach not only generates innovative solutions but also strengthens team cohesion and engagement.

Uncertainty can create anxiety, especially if team members are unclear about how changes might affect them. As a leader, one of your most powerful tools in these situations is transparent communication. Be honest about what you know, acknowledge what remains uncertain, and explain how you plan to address the challenges. Transparency reassures your team that you're handling the situation openly and ethically, building trust and a sense of security.

While transparency is essential, projecting confidence is equally important. Even if you don't have all the answers, your composure and clarity signal stability. A leader who remains calm and focused inspires the same in their team. Confidence in uncertain times isn't about pretending to have it all figured out; it's about trusting in your ability to adapt, make thoughtful decisions, and lead with integrity.

For instance, if a project is delayed due to unforeseen circumstances, be upfront with your team. Explain the factors causing the delay, outline the steps you're taking to address the issue, and express confidence in the team's ability to navigate the situation together. This combination of transparency and reassurance keeps your team motivated, focused, and resilient.

Every decision made during uncertain times offers a valuable opportunity to grow. After the decision has played out, take time to evaluate the outcomes and reflect on the lessons learned. Consider what worked well, what could have been improved, and how you might handle similar situations differently in the future. This intentional reflection not only strengthens your decision-making skills but also enhances your ability to adapt to challenges with greater confidence.

Involve your team in this reflection process by inviting their feedback on the decision and its impact. Ask them about their experience with the process—what they found effective and what they think could be refined. This collective learning approach fosters a growth-oriented culture where challenges are seen not as setbacks but as opportunities for development. It signals to your team that their insights matter and that growth is a shared journey.

By continuously refining your approach, you build resilience and a sense of preparedness, both for yourself and your team. Each decision becomes a stepping stone, contributing to your collective ability to navigate future uncertainty with clarity and strength.

Decision-making during uncertain times is a unique skill— a balance of flexibility, empathy, and courage. While uncertainty can't be eliminated, it can be managed through thoughtful strategies that prioritize values, adaptability, and transparent communication. By leading with a steady hand and an open mind, you inspire confidence in your team, helping them stay focused, united, and resilient as they face challenges together.

Evaluating and Learning from Decisions

Decision-making doesn't end once a choice is made. In leadership, every decision is a stepping stone for growth, learning, and improvement. By taking the time to evaluate past decisions, leaders gain valuable insights into what went well, what could have been done differently, and how future choices can be refined. Reflection strengthens self-awareness and creates a framework for more thoughtful decision-making over time.

Evaluating decisions fosters accountability and resilience. It shifts the mindset from seeing outcomes as fixed successes or failures to viewing them as learning opportunities. Leaders who prioritize this reflective practice set a powerful example, showing their teams that challenges are opportunities to grow, adapt, and innovate.

Establishing a structured process for evaluating decisions ensures that reflection becomes a deliberate habit rather than an afterthought. Schedule regular review sessions after major decisions, whether as one-on-one reflections or team discussions, depending on the decision's scope and impact. Making evaluation a routine practice encourages deeper insights and thoughtful learning.

- During these sessions, use key questions to guide the conversation:
- What was the outcome of the decision? Did it meet our expectations?
- What worked well during the decision-making process?

- What challenges or obstacles arose, and how were they handled?
- Were there any unintended consequences, and how did we address them?
- What could have been done differently to achieve a better result?

These questions provide a framework for dissecting the decision, allowing you to analyze both the process and its outcomes. By breaking it down, you uncover actionable insights that refine your approach to future challenges.

Team feedback is an essential part of decision evaluation. Team members bring unique perspectives on how decisions impact their work, morale, and overall dynamics. Their input adds depth to your understanding and reinforces a culture of collaboration and continuous improvement.

Encourage your team to share their thoughts by asking open-ended questions like:

- How did the decision affect your work or the team's performance?
- Did you feel informed and supported throughout the process?
- What suggestions do you have for improving future decision-making?

Inviting feedback shows your team that their opinions matter and that their experiences influence how decisions are shaped going forward. This openness builds trust and encourages a collaborative spirit, where team members feel invested in both the process and its outcomes.

By creating a feedback loop, you strengthen your team's connection to leadership and reinforce a growth mindset across the organization. Every decision becomes more than a singular event—it becomes an opportunity to learn, improve, and lead with greater purpose.

Reviewing past decisions often reveals patterns that provide valuable insights into your decision-making style. Perhaps you notice a tendency to rely heavily on data or prefer quick decisions in certain situations. Recognizing these patterns helps you understand your strengths and identify areas for improvement— whether it's slowing down to gather more input or incorporating more intuition into data-heavy decisions.

Each decision is an opportunity to identify lessons that strengthen your framework. For instance, if a decision didn't meet expectations due to insufficient planning, you might commit to allocating more preparation time in the future. Conversely, if a collaborative approach led to a particularly successful outcome, it's a signal to involve your team early on more consistently.

These insights serve as guideposts for your ongoing development as a leader. By learning from each decision, you refine your approach, becoming more adaptable and confident over time. The cumulative effect of these lessons enhances your leadership effectiveness and strengthens your ability to make thoughtful, purpose-driven decisions.

The ultimate goal of evaluating decisions is to improve future choices. Use the lessons learned to inform your approach and adjust as needed. For example, if clear communication during a previous decision enhanced team alignment, make transparency a priority in your next process. If consulting with stakeholders proved valuable, incorporate it as a standard practice going forward.

Consider documenting these insights in a checklist or playbook of best practices that evolves with experience. This guide can serve as a quick reference, reminding you of key elements like consulting the team, balancing data and intuition, or preparing contingency plans. By applying these lessons consistently, you create a feedback loop that elevates your decision-making process, reinforcing a culture of continuous improvement within your team.

Reflection and feedback are cornerstones of a culture of continuous improvement. When leaders model this approach, they encourage their teams to embrace growth-oriented thinking. This mindset shifts the focus from perfection to progress, valuing both successes and setbacks as opportunities to learn.

Encourage your team to reflect on their decisions and share their insights. Create regular opportunities for open dialogue about what worked, what didn't, and what can be improved. For example, consider holding monthly or quarterly "lessons learned" meetings where team members can discuss recent projects and decisions. These discussions foster transparency, collective growth, and innovation.

By promoting this culture, you build resilience and adaptability within your team, equipping them to navigate challenges and continuously enhance their performance.

Evaluation isn't just about identifying areas for improvement—it's also an opportunity to celebrate growth and progress. Acknowledge decisions that led to positive outcomes, and recognize the collaboration and effort that contributed to those successes.

When a challenging decision results in a win, share the achievement with your team and reflect on the factors that led to the success. Celebrating these moments reinforces the value of thoughtful decision-making and boosts team morale. This recognition encourages ongoing engagement, reminding your team that their contributions matter and that success is a shared achievement.

Evaluating and learning from decisions is a cornerstone of leadership growth. By reflecting on outcomes, gathering feedback, identifying patterns, and celebrating progress, you refine your decision-making skills and cultivate a culture of continuous improvement. Each decision becomes a stepping stone in a learning journey, helping you lead with greater confidence and inspiring your team to strive for excellence.

Building Emotional Intelligence

Understanding Emotional Intelligence and Its Importance in Leadership

Emotional Intelligence (EI) is the ability to recognize, understand, and manage your own emotions while also perceiving, understanding, and influencing the emotions of others. Often described as a defining trait of effective leaders, EI enables the cultivation of strong relationships, the empathetic navigation of challenges, and the creation of positive team dynamics. Leaders with high emotional intelligence exhibit self-awareness, empathy, and interpersonal skills that build trust, motivation, and open communication within their teams.

In leadership, EI influences every interaction and decision. By attuning to their own emotions and those of their team, leaders foster an environment of understanding and respect. This emotional awareness is particularly vital in managing conflict, guiding team members through challenges, and addressing difficult situations. Leaders with strong EI create loyalty, resilience, and a shared sense of purpose, driving both individual and team growth.

Emotional intelligence is often divided into five key components, each essential for effective leadership:

Self-Awareness: Recognizing your own emotions, strengths, limitations, and values and understanding how they influence your behavior. Self-aware leaders manage their reactions effectively, maintain composure under stress, and lead with authenticity.

Self-Regulation: Managing emotions in a constructive way, enabling thoughtful responses rather than impulsive reactions. Leaders who self-regulate remain calm, adaptable, and resilient, even in high-pressure scenarios.

Motivation: The internal drive to achieve goals, pursue excellence, and maintain a positive outlook despite setbacks. Highly motivated leaders inspire themselves and their teams to stay proactive and purpose-driven.

Empathy: Understanding and sharing the feelings of others. Empathetic leaders build trust and rapport by connecting with their team on a personal level and addressing their needs with genuine understanding.

Social Skills: Building and maintaining healthy relationships, communicating effectively, and resolving conflicts. Leaders with strong social skills foster collaboration, create positive environments, and navigate complex team dynamics seamlessly.

By cultivating these core components, leaders enhance their ability to connect with, inspire, and guide their teams toward success.

EI shapes a leader's effectiveness and team culture profoundly. Leaders with high EI are more adaptable, open-minded, and resilient—qualities critical in today's dynamic work environments. EI enables leaders to make balanced decisions by considering both logical and emotional aspects, resulting in choices that are effective and empathetic.

Emotionally intelligent leaders excel in communication, expressing ideas and feedback in ways that resonate. By understanding their own emotions and those of their team, they foster psychological safety, where team members feel empowered to share ideas and address concerns. This openness drives collaboration, trust, and innovation.

Additionally, leaders with strong EI handle stress effectively. By managing their emotions during challenges, they provide stability and reassurance, encouraging their team to face obstacles with confidence. This composure reinforces a solution-oriented culture and creates a resilient team dynamic.

The foundation of EI lies in self-awareness and self-regulation. Self-aware leaders recognize emotional triggers, strengths, and weaknesses, enabling intentional responses rather than impulsive reactions.

Building Self-Awareness:

Set aside time for reflection to evaluate emotional responses to various situations.

Ask reflective questions, such as:

What emotions influenced my interactions this week?

Did I react impulsively, and how could I have responded better?

What strengths did I demonstrate, and what areas need improvement?

Practicing Self-Regulation:

Use techniques like mindfulness, deep breathing, or taking a pause before responding to manage stress effectively.

Model calmness and resilience, setting a tone that encourages your team to adopt similar behaviors.

Empathy allows leaders to connect deeply with their teams, fostering trust and engagement. Empathetic leaders understand their team members' challenges and aspirations, responding in ways that build rapport and motivation.

Actively listen and observe nonverbal cues, such as tone and body language.

Ask perspective-taking questions like:

What might this person be feeling?

How can I support them effectively?

Small empathetic actions, such as acknowledging efforts or offering assistance, strengthen team bonds and cultivate a supportive environment.

Strong social skills enable leaders to foster collaboration, resolve conflicts, and build cohesive teams.

Communication: Practice clear, consistent messaging that reinforces understanding and expectations. Use both verbal and nonverbal cues to convey sincerity and clarity.

Conflict Resolution: Address conflicts with empathy and a focus on solutions. Facilitate open dialogue and encourage mutual understanding, creating trust and cooperation.

By leveraging social skills, leaders create an inclusive, high-performing team culture where everyone feels valued and motivated.

Emotional intelligence is a cornerstone of effective leadership. Leaders who develop self-awareness, self-regulation, empathy, and social skills foster stronger relationships, create positive team dynamics, and navigate challenges with resilience. By prioritizing EI, leaders build a supportive, engaging environment that empowers their teams to thrive and succeed.

Developing Self-Awareness and Self-Management

Self-awareness and self-management are at the core of emotional intelligence, providing leaders with the insight and control needed to respond thoughtfully rather than react impulsively. Self-awareness is the ability to recognize and understand your emotions, strengths, and areas for improvement. Self-management, on the other hand, is the skill of regulating your emotions, maintaining control in challenging situations, and adapting to change. Together, these abilities allow leaders to approach situations with composure, make more rational decisions, and build trust and respect within their teams.

Mastering self-awareness and self-management requires regular reflection and a commitment to understanding how emotions influence your behavior and decisions. By developing these skills, leaders can create a stable, grounded presence that inspires confidence and fosters a supportive team environment.

Self-awareness begins with a willingness to look inward and examine your emotions, reactions, and motivations. Leaders who are self-aware understand how their emotions affect their behavior and interactions, enabling them to make more intentional choices. Developing self-awareness involves both reflection and the ability to observe your responses in real-time.

A practical way to build self-awareness is through regular reflection. Set aside time each day or week to assess your emotional responses to various situations. Consider questions like:

What emotions did I experience today, and how did they impact my behavior?

Were there any moments when I reacted impulsively? How could I have handled them differently?

What strengths did I demonstrate, and what areas could use improvement?

Journaling can be a helpful tool for reflection. Writing down your experiences and emotions allows you to identify patterns, recognize triggers, and track your progress over time. Over weeks and months, this reflective practice helps you develop a deeper understanding of your emotional landscape, enabling you to respond with greater awareness in the future.

An essential aspect of self-awareness is identifying emotional triggers—situations, people, or environments that tend to provoke strong emotional reactions. By recognizing your triggers, you gain the power to manage your responses rather than allowing emotions to control your actions. This self-knowledge helps you approach challenging situations calmly and thoughtfully, setting a positive example for your team.

To identify triggers, think back to recent moments when you experienced heightened emotions. What were the circumstances? How did you react? For instance, you might notice that unexpected changes or tight deadlines create stress and lead to impulsive reactions. By becoming aware of these triggers, you can prepare yourself to respond more effectively when similar situations arise.

Once you've identified your triggers, consider ways to manage your response. For example, if tight deadlines create stress, develop a practice of taking a few deep breaths or a short pause before responding. This momentary break allows you to regain control of your emotions, making it easier to respond with composure.

Self-management is the ability to control your emotions and reactions, maintaining a steady demeanor even when facing pressure. Leaders who practice self-management inspire trust, as they demonstrate a level of resilience and reliability that their team can depend on. Self-management is particularly valuable in high-stress situations, where maintaining composure can make the difference between a positive and negative outcome.

One of the most effective ways to build self-management skills is by practicing mindfulness. Mindfulness involves focusing on the present moment without judgment, allowing you to observe your emotions and thoughts without reacting impulsively. When you're mindful, you create space between an emotional trigger and your response, giving yourself the opportunity to choose how to act.

For example, if you receive unexpected feedback that provokes a strong emotional response, practice taking a few deep breaths and pausing before replying. This mindful pause allows you to process your emotions, consider the feedback objectively, and respond constructively. Over time, mindfulness strengthens your ability to regulate emotions, reducing impulsive reactions and helping you navigate challenges calmly.

Other self-management techniques include:

Setting Personal Boundaries: Establish limits on your time, energy, and attention, ensuring that you're not overcommitting yourself. Setting boundaries helps you manage stress and prevent burnout, supporting long-term emotional stability.

Practicing Positive Self-Talk: Replace self-critical thoughts with encouraging, constructive messages. For example, instead of thinking, "I can't handle this," try saying, "This is challenging, but I'm capable of finding a solution." Positive self-talk reinforces a growth mindset and bolsters resilience.

Managing Your Environment: When possible, create an environment that supports emotional balance. If a particular setting or person tends to provoke stress, find ways to minimize exposure or implement practices that help you manage these interactions with confidence.

Self-management also involves learning to adapt to changing circumstances with flexibility. In leadership, situations can change quickly, and being able to adjust your plans and expectations without becoming frustrated is an essential skill. Practice viewing unexpected changes as opportunities for growth rather than setbacks, focusing on how you can respond constructively.

Leaders who are self-aware and manage their emotions

effectively create an atmosphere of trust within their team. When team members see that their leader can handle challenges calmly and constructively, they feel more secure, knowing that they're working with someone who prioritizes stability and fairness. This sense of trust encourages team members to approach their leader with concerns, share honest feedback, and collaborate openly.

To build trust, practice sharing your own self-awareness journey with your team. For instance, if you're working on managing stress or improving communication, let your team know. By sharing your commitment to self-improvement, you demonstrate vulnerability and openness, qualities that make you more relatable and approachable. When your team sees that you're committed to personal growth, they're more likely to adopt a similar approach, contributing to a culture of continuous improvement.

Additionally, use self-awareness and self-management to create an emotionally safe environment. When team members experience setbacks, respond with empathy and support rather than criticism. By modeling patience and understanding, you set a tone of respect and acceptance, making it easier for team members to bring their full selves to work without fear of judgment.

As with any skill, developing self-awareness and self-management takes time and consistent effort. Track your progress by reflecting on specific situations where you applied these skills effectively. For instance, if you managed to remain calm during a difficult meeting or successfully redirected an impulsive reaction, take a moment to acknowledge this growth. Recognizing small victories reinforces your commitment to emotional intelligence, motivating you to continue developing these skills.

Celebrate growth with your team as well. When you model self-awareness and self-management effectively, acknowledge the positive impact it has on the team dynamic. By openly valuing these skills, you encourage team members to prioritize their own emotional intelligence, building a culture that values self-improvement, resilience, and mutual respect.

Self-awareness and self-management are the foundations of emotional intelligence, enabling leaders to navigate their emotions with control and clarity. By developing these skills, you build a leadership style that is grounded, empathetic, and adaptable, inspiring your team to bring their best selves to work and creating a supportive environment where everyone can thrive.

Practicing Empathy in Leadership

Empathy is more than just understanding someone's feelings—it's about connecting with them on a human level. For leaders, this isn't optional; it's essential. When you practice empathy, you build bridges of trust and create a culture where people feel seen, heard, and valued. You go beyond the surface and connect with your team in a way that fosters loyalty, motivation, and genuine engagement.

Empathy in leadership isn't just listening to concerns or nodding along. It's about leaning in with intention, understanding perspectives, and responding in a way that says, "I'm here, and I care." When leaders do this consistently, they transform workplaces into environments of respect, support, and collaboration. It's this connection that turns "just a job" into something meaningful—for everyone involved.

Empathy is a game-changer in leadership. Why? Because it builds trust. When people know you genuinely care about them—not just their output—they're more willing to open up, take risks, and share ideas. This trust is the foundation of collaboration and innovation.

Empathy also elevates communication. When you're attuned to the emotions behind someone's words, your responses are more thoughtful, more human. You're not just addressing the issue; you're addressing the person. This kind of emotional insight fosters stronger bonds and clarity, making misunderstandings less likely.

And let's not overlook morale. When people feel like they matter, they show up differently. Empathy inspires commitment because it communicates that every person, every role, has value. It's a powerful motivator that aligns individual efforts with collective success.

Empathy starts with listening—not the kind where you're just waiting for your turn to speak, but the kind where you're fully present. Put the phone down, make eye contact, and really hear what's being said (and sometimes, what isn't).

When someone comes to you with a concern or idea, don't rush to respond. Take a beat. Nod. Ask questions like, "Can you tell me more about how that's been affecting you?" Reflect back what you're hearing: "It sounds like you're feeling overwhelmed because of the tight deadline. Is that right?" This doesn't just show that you're paying attention; it shows you care enough to understand.

Here's the trick: often, people don't need you to fix it. They need you to get it. Listening without judgment or interruption creates the space for people to feel safe and valued. And when people feel safe, they thrive.

Empathy means imagining what it's like to stand where someone else stands. Maybe it's a team member who's juggling work and personal challenges. Or maybe it's someone frustrated by a lack of resources. The question to ask yourself is: What might they be feeling right now?

This doesn't mean you have to agree with every point or accommodate every need. But by stepping into their shoes— even briefly—you gain insight into what's driving their emotions. That understanding alone can change the way you respond.

Let's say a team member seems withdrawn in meetings.

Instead of writing it off as disinterest, consider what might be causing it. Are they overwhelmed? Feeling unheard? When you take the time to explore what's beneath the surface, you're better positioned to offer meaningful support.

Empathy is a verb. It's not just about what you feel; it's about what you do with that feeling. When someone shares a challenge, respond in a way that shows you've heard them. Maybe it's adjusting their workload, offering a flexible schedule, or simply saying, "I appreciate what you're going through, and I'm here if you need anything."

Compassion doesn't have to be complicated. Sometimes, it's as simple as acknowledging effort: "I know this project has been a heavy lift. Thank you for sticking with it." These small moments of recognition add up, creating an environment where people feel supported and motivated.

You can't connect with others if you're out of touch with yourself. Empathy starts with self-awareness—recognizing your emotions and how they influence your interactions. Are you stressed? Frustrated? Excited? Knowing where you're at emotionally helps you show up authentically and with intention.

It's equally important to manage those emotions. Leadership isn't about being emotionless; it's about channeling your emotions effectively. Before reacting to a tense situation, take a breath. Center yourself. This doesn't just help you; it sets the tone for your team.

Empathy is contagious. When you model it, your team picks up on it. They start to show the same care and respect to each other. Suddenly, you're not just leading a team; you're shaping a culture—one that values people as much as outcomes.

Encourage empathy by fostering connection. Create opportunities for team members to share their experiences, whether through regular check-ins, team-building activities, or open forums. And when you see acts of empathy within the team, call them out. Celebrate them. This reinforces that empathy isn't just a leadership trait—it's a team value.

Empathy is more than a leadership skill; it's a way of being. It's what turns managers into mentors and colleagues into collaborators. When you lead with empathy, you create a workplace where people feel seen, respected, and inspired to give their best. That's the kind of leadership that leaves a legacy—one built on connection, trust, and shared purpose.

Enhancing Social Skills for Better Collaboration

Social skills are the bridge that connects emotional intelligence with effective teamwork. They enable leaders to communicate clearly, build trust, resolve conflicts, and foster positive relationships. Strong social skills make it easier for leaders to navigate team dynamics, creating an environment where collaboration and mutual respect thrive. Leaders with well-developed social skills know how to motivate their team, manage differences constructively, and inspire a shared sense of purpose.

For leaders, social skills are more than just tools for communication; they are the foundation of a cohesive, high-performing team. By developing these skills, you empower your team to contribute openly, support one another, and stay engaged with collective goals. Enhancing social skills involves a combination of empathy, clear communication, and conflict resolution techniques that enable you to lead with both warmth and authority.

Effective communication is at the heart of successful leadership. Leaders who communicate clearly and openly set the stage for a team culture built on trust, respect, and mutual understanding. Strong communication involves not only speaking effectively but also listening attentively, recognizing nonverbal cues, and ensuring that each message is understood as intended.

To enhance communication, practice expressing your ideas and instructions clearly and concisely. Avoid jargon or ambiguous language, opting instead for straightforward terms that leave no room for misinterpretation. For instance, instead of saying, "We need to improve this process," specify what improvements are expected, such as, "Let's aim to streamline steps three and four to reduce the overall project time."

Active listening is equally important. When team members speak, give them your full attention, avoid interrupting, and ask clarifying questions to confirm your understanding. This attentiveness demonstrates respect for their input, encouraging open dialogue and ensuring that all perspectives are considered. By fostering a culture of open communication, you make it easier for team members to share ideas, voice concerns, and collaborate effectively.

Conflict is a natural part of any collaborative environment, and effective leaders know how to address it constructively. When handled well, conflicts can lead to growth, innovation, and stronger relationships. Leaders who approach conflicts with empathy, fairness, and a focus on resolution create a space where team members feel safe to express differences and work through disagreements respectfully.

To resolve conflicts constructively, start by understanding the root cause. Rather than addressing only the surface-level disagreement, explore the underlying issues or emotions that may be contributing to the tension. For example, if two team members disagree on a project approach, ask open-ended questions to understand each person's perspective fully. "Can you share more about why you feel this approach is best?" or "What concerns do you have about the current plan?" These questions encourage each party to articulate their thoughts and feelings, which often brings clarity to the issue.

Once both perspectives are clear, facilitate a discussion

that focuses on finding common ground and identifying solutions. Encourage team members to suggest compromises or adjustments that address their concerns. This collaborative approach not only resolves the immediate conflict but also builds trust, as team members see that their viewpoints are valued and respected. By guiding the team through conflict with empathy and patience, you model a positive, respectful approach to handling differences.

Relationship-building is essential for creating a team culture where collaboration feels natural and rewarding. Leaders who invest time in getting to know their team members on a personal level create a sense of connection that strengthens trust and morale. Positive relationships make team members feel valued, fostering an environment where they're motivated to contribute, support one another, and work toward shared goals.

Building relationships starts with showing genuine interest in your team members' experiences, strengths, and aspirations. Take time to engage in one-on-one conversations, asking questions about their interests, goals, and challenges. This practice of getting to know each team member individually not only strengthens your bond with them but also provides valuable insights into their motivations and potential areas for growth.

Additionally, create opportunities for team members to connect with each other. Encourage team-building activities, whether it's informal gatherings, collaborative projects, or discussions where people can share their ideas and experiences. By fostering a sense of camaraderie, you build a team culture where collaboration feels seamless and rewarding, making it easier for everyone to work together productively.

Openness and transparency are vital for building trust and engagement. Leaders who communicate transparently about decisions, goals, and challenges demonstrate that they value their team's input and respect their need for clarity. When team members feel informed, they're more likely to stay engaged, motivated, and aligned with the team's objectives.

Practice transparency by sharing relevant information with your team, whether it's about organizational changes, project updates, or upcoming challenges. When you make decisions that affect the team, explain the reasoning behind them. This openness creates a culture of trust, as team members see that you're committed to keeping them in the loop.

Encourage your team to adopt the same level of openness with each other. Create a safe space for sharing ideas, asking questions, and providing feedback without fear of judgment. This culture of transparency fosters a supportive, respectful environment where everyone feels empowered to contribute their best and collaborate effectively.

As a leader, your social skills set the tone for how team members interact with one another. By modeling positive social behaviors—such as active listening, respect, and patience—you encourage your team to adopt these qualities as well. Leading by example creates a ripple effect, as team members observe your approach and mirror it in their own interactions.

For instance, if you consistently handle conflicts with empathy and fairness, team members are more likely to do the same. If you prioritize open communication and express appreciation for their efforts, they'll be inspired to adopt similar practices. This consistent modeling of positive social skills reinforces a team culture where collaboration, respect, and trust are core values.

Additionally, acknowledge and celebrate when team members demonstrate strong social skills. Recognize acts of kindness, support, or collaborative problem-solving, and let the team know that you value these contributions. Positive reinforcement strengthens the team's commitment to healthy social interactions, creating a cohesive and high-performing group.

Social skills, like any other leadership skill, require practice and continuous improvement. Seek feedback from your team on your communication style, conflict-resolution approach, and overall interaction with them. Use this feedback to refine your social skills, ensuring that you're meeting the team's needs and setting a positive example.

Consider taking time each month to reflect on your recent interactions. Ask yourself questions like:

Did I communicate clearly and effectively?

How did I handle recent conflicts, and could I have approached them differently?

Are there areas where I could improve in building relationships and fostering team cohesion?

By actively reflecting on your social skills and seeking opportunities to improve, you reinforce your commitment to becoming a more effective, empathetic leader. This dedication to growth inspires your team to do the same, creating a culture where everyone values self-improvement and positive interactions.

Enhancing social skills empowers you to lead with empathy, clarity, and respect. By mastering communication, resolving conflicts constructively, fostering positive relationships, and leading by example, you create a collaborative environment where each team member feels valued and motivated. These social skills are the building blocks of a cohesive, engaged team that is equipped to achieve collective success.

Building Resilience and Managing Stress

Resilience is the ability to bounce back from setbacks, adapt to challenges, and maintain a positive outlook amid adversity. For leaders, it's a cornerstone of maintaining focus, inspiring confidence, and guiding a team through difficult times. Equally important is managing stress, as unchecked stress can cloud judgment, hinder decision-making, and strain interactions with team members. Leaders who prioritize resilience and stress management foster a stable, supportive environment where their teams feel empowered to tackle challenges with optimism and determination.

Building resilience doesn't mean ignoring stress or pushing through challenges without support. Instead, it involves adopting habits and perspectives that help you respond constructively to stressors, learn from setbacks, and grow stronger with every experience. By fostering resilience in yourself, you set the tone for your team to do the same, creating a culture that values persistence, adaptability, and emotional well-being.

A positive mindset is the foundation of resilience. Leaders who approach challenges with optimism and a solution-focused attitude are better equipped to handle setbacks and stress. This doesn't mean ignoring difficulties; rather, it's about focusing on potential solutions, opportunities for growth, and what's within your control.

Reframe challenges as opportunities. If a project faces delays, shift the focus from frustration to how the extra time can enhance quality or address potential issues. This perspective fosters a proactive, constructive approach that reduces stress and reinforces resilience.

Practicing gratitude is another way to strengthen positivity. Each day, take a moment to acknowledge what's going well or reflect on your team's progress. Gratitude helps shift your attention away from stressors and reminds you of the strengths and achievements that fuel your leadership journey.

Effective stress management is key to maintaining resilience and composure. When left unchecked, stress can undermine focus, patience, and decision-making. Proactively managing stress ensures that you're able to lead with clarity and strength, even in high-pressure situations.

Consider integrating these strategies into your routine:

Mindfulness and Deep Breathing: Staying present through mindfulness reduces anxiety about future uncertainties. Simple breathing exercises can calm your nervous system, helping you approach challenges with a clear mind.

Physical Activity: Regular exercise relieves stress and boosts energy. Even short walks or quick stretches during the day can enhance mood and focus.

Setting Boundaries: Protect your personal time and energy by saying no to unnecessary commitments. Healthy boundaries prevent burnout and allow you to recharge.

Time Management: Break large tasks into manageable steps and prioritize effectively. A well-organized schedule reduces overwhelm and keeps you in control.

By embedding these techniques into your daily routine, you're better prepared to handle challenges with calmness and resilience.

Resilience often flourishes with support. A strong network—both within and beyond your team—provides encouragement, fresh perspectives, and practical help when times get tough. Trusted colleagues, mentors, or friends can offer guidance, share insights, or simply listen when you need to process emotions.

Within your team, create a culture of mutual support by encouraging open communication and acknowledging each other's efforts. When team members trust one another, they approach challenges collaboratively, reinforcing resilience as a group dynamic.

Outside your team, connect with mentors or peers who understand the pressures of leadership. Their advice and reassurance can help you navigate uncertainty, providing the clarity needed to stay grounded.

Resilient leaders view setbacks as opportunities to learn and grow. Each challenge offers insights that can refine your approach and prepare you for the future. Instead of dwelling on mistakes, focus on the lessons they provide.

When a setback occurs, reflect by asking:

What contributed to this outcome, and what could I have done differently?

What did I learn about myself, my team, or the situation?

How can I apply these lessons moving forward?

Adaptability is another cornerstone of resilience. In dynamic work environments, circumstances shift quickly. Leaders who embrace change with curiosity and optimism inspire their teams to remain flexible and focused. Treat change as an opportunity to innovate, and guide your team to see its potential rather than its challenges.

Ambitious goals drive success, but unrealistic expectations can lead to unnecessary stress. Resilient leaders strike a balance by setting achievable goals that challenge their team without overwhelming them. Breaking large objectives into smaller milestones helps maintain motivation and provides a sense of accomplishment, even in long-term projects.

When setbacks occur, adjust expectations and focus on what's still possible. Communicate these adjusted goals transparently, emphasizing that success is a journey, not a single destination. This approach fosters patience and perseverance, both essential for resilience.

Your approach to resilience sets the tone for your team. By demonstrating composure, adaptability, and optimism, you inspire confidence and encourage others to follow suit. Transparency is key—acknowledge challenges openly, but focus on solutions and next steps. This balanced approach builds trust and shows that you're capable of leading through adversity.

Celebrate moments of perseverance and growth within your team. Recognize their efforts in overcoming challenges or adapting to change. This reinforcement strengthens their commitment to resilience and reinforces its value in achieving shared success.

Building resilience and managing stress are integral to effective leadership. By cultivating a positive mindset, mastering stress management, nurturing a support network, and modeling resilience, you create a foundation for stability and strength. These qualities not only enhance your leadership but also empower your team to face challenges with determination and optimism. Together, you build a culture of growth, adaptability, and success.

Building A Vision and Setting Goals

Crafting a Compelling Vision for Your Team

A compelling vision is the cornerstone of effective leadership. It gives your team direction, purpose, and a sense of unity, serving as a guiding light for their efforts. A well-defined vision doesn't just outline what the team aims to achieve—it explains why it matters. Leaders who articulate a clear and inspiring vision create a culture of purpose, motivating their teams to give their best with enthusiasm and commitment.

Creating a vision isn't just about setting goals. It's about understanding the team's values, strengths, and aspirations and framing them in a way that resonates with everyone. A strong vision connects daily tasks to a bigger, impactful purpose, empowering your team to find deeper meaning in their work. By crafting a vision that appeals to both logic and emotion, you inspire loyalty and drive that lasts far beyond any single milestone.

Every vision begins with purpose—the why behind your team's work. Purpose gives meaning to what the team does, highlighting the value it brings to the organization, customers, or community. When leaders communicate a clear and meaningful purpose, they inspire pride and intrinsic motivation.

Start by asking yourself:

What unique value does our team bring?

What positive impact do we want to create through our work?

What values guide our decisions and interactions?

Along with purpose, establish core values that shape how the team works toward its goals. These values—like collaboration, integrity, innovation, or customer focus—serve as guideposts for decisions and behaviors. They provide stability and clarity, especially during challenging times.

For example, if your team's purpose is to develop innovative solutions that improve customer experiences, align this with values like creativity, customer-centricity, and adaptability. When purpose and values work hand-in-hand, they create a vision that's both emotionally resonant and practically actionable.

With your purpose and values in place, paint a vivid picture of what success looks like. A compelling vision should describe a future that's ambitious enough to inspire, yet grounded enough to feel achievable. It should excite your team about what's possible while giving them confidence that they can make it happen.

To craft this future state, ask:

What does success look like in the next few years?

How will achieving this vision impact our organization, customers, or community?

What will be different once we've reached our goals?

Don't just focus on numbers or metrics—tell a story that makes the vision come alive. For instance, instead of saying, "Our goal is to increase efficiency by 20%," try, "Imagine a team where every process flows seamlessly, freeing us up to focus on bold, creative projects that delight our customers and drive innovation." A vision rooted in both emotional and practical outcomes will resonate more deeply with your team.

A vision is most powerful when team members see themselves in it. When it aligns with their personal goals, strengths, and passions, they'll feel more connected and invested in making it a reality.

Take the time to understand what drives each member of your team. Ask:

What part of our work excites you most?

What goals do you have for your growth within the team?

How do you want to contribute to the team's success?

Use these insights to personalize the vision. Show individuals how their unique contributions are essential to achieving the broader goal. For example, if someone values innovation, emphasize how their creativity will help shape new solutions. When team members feel their aspirations are tied to the team's purpose, they'll work with greater motivation and pride.

A vision gains strength through communication. Leaders who share their vision clearly, consistently, and passionately ensure that it becomes an integral part of the team's culture.

When introducing the vision, use straightforward, relatable language. Avoid jargon or overly complex terms. Instead, focus on connecting the vision to the team's values and daily efforts. Use stories, visuals, or examples to make the vision tangible and memorable.

Reinforce the vision regularly. Refer back to it in team meetings, one-on-ones, and project updates. Celebrate progress by tying achievements to the vision, helping the team see how their work contributes to the bigger picture. Consistent communication keeps the vision alive, ensuring it remains a central focus.

A vision is only as powerful as the leader behind it. When you embody the vision through your actions and decisions, you show the team that you're genuinely committed to its success. This authenticity inspires trust and alignment.

Living the vision means demonstrating the values and behaviors it represents. For example, if the vision prioritizes innovation, lead by example: encourage creative thinking, take calculated risks, and recognize bold ideas. If the vision emphasizes customer focus, go out of your way to highlight and reward excellent service.

Your energy and enthusiasm set the tone. Stay optimistic and solution-focused, even in the face of challenges. When team members see your unwavering belief in the vision, they're more likely to adopt it as their own and stay committed to achieving it.

A compelling vision is a powerful force for unity and motivation. By defining a clear purpose, imagining an inspiring future state, aligning with team members' aspirations, communicating consistently, and leading by example, you create a team that's connected, driven, and ready to achieve great things. A well-crafted vision isn't just a statement—it's a shared journey that brings people together, transforming day-to-day work into something meaningful and impactful.

Setting SMART Goals for Team Success

A compelling vision lays the groundwork for your team's purpose, but specific, actionable goals are what turn that vision into reality. SMART goals—Specific, Measurable, Achievable, Relevant, and Time-bound—bridge the gap between aspiration and execution. They provide clarity, foster accountability, and motivate your team by giving them a clear roadmap to success. Leaders who set SMART goals cultivate a culture of achievement, focus, and continuous growth.

Effective goal-setting begins with aligning goals to the team's vision and breaking larger objectives into manageable, actionable steps. By leveraging the SMART framework, you ensure that every goal is clear, purpose-driven, and achievable, helping your team focus on what truly matters. SMART goals empower individuals to take ownership of their contributions while providing a structure for tracking progress and celebrating success.

The first element of a SMART goal is specificity. Specific goals eliminate ambiguity, making it clear exactly what needs to be accomplished. Without specificity, team members may struggle to understand expectations, leading to inefficiencies and missed opportunities. A specific goal provides focus, enabling effective action.

To make goals specific, address the what, why, and how. For instance, instead of saying, "Improve team performance," define the target: "Increase the team's project completion rate by 15% over the next six months to better meet client expectations." This version specifies the desired outcome, timeframe, and purpose, creating a clear and actionable target.

Ask yourself:

What exactly do we want to achieve?

Who is responsible for achieving it?

What specific steps are required?

By defining goals with precision, you create a shared understanding that keeps everyone aligned and moving in the same direction.

Measurable goals provide a way to track progress and gauge success. They include concrete criteria or metrics, allowing the team to see how far they've come and what remains to be done. Clear measurement fosters accountability and keeps motivation high, as progress becomes visible and tangible.

To make goals measurable, determine the metrics or benchmarks that will define success. For example, if the goal is to improve customer satisfaction, specify a target: "Achieve a customer satisfaction score of 90% or higher within the next quarter." This measurable goal gives the team a clear benchmark to work toward.

Consider:

What metrics will define success?

How will we track progress over time?

What tools or methods will we use to measure outcomes?

Measurable goals not only provide clarity but also offer valuable insights, enabling the team to identify strengths and address areas for improvement.

Goals should challenge your team, but they must also be realistic. Achievable goals balance ambition with practicality, taking into account available resources, skills, and constraints. Unrealistic goals can lead to frustration and burnout, while achievable ones build momentum and confidence.

Evaluate the team's current capabilities when setting goals. For instance, if the objective is to launch a new product, assess whether the timeline and resources align with the project's scope. A more achievable version might be, "Develop a prototype of the new product within the next quarter, with contributions from both design and marketing teams." This goal pushes the team while remaining within reach.

Ask:

Can this goal be realistically accomplished with our resources?

Do team members have the skills or support needed?

What challenges might arise, and how can we address them?

By setting achievable goals, you foster a sense of progress and ensure that your team remains motivated.

Relevance ensures that goals contribute meaningfully to the team's vision and priorities. Relevant goals prevent distractions, focusing energy on what truly drives success. They connect the work of individuals to the broader purpose, reinforcing a shared sense of direction.

Evaluate the relevance of each goal by asking:

Does this goal support our team's vision and values?

How will achieving it contribute to the organization's success?

Is this goal a priority compared to others?

For example, if your vision emphasizes sustainability, a relevant goal might be, "Reduce production waste by 20% over the next year to align with our commitment to sustainable practices." This goal ties directly to the vision, creating a sense of purpose and alignment.

Time-bound goals provide deadlines that create urgency and help prioritize tasks. A specific timeframe clarifies expectations, ensuring that team members can plan their efforts and track progress effectively. Time-bound goals also drive momentum, keeping the team engaged as they work toward a clear endpoint.

To set time-bound goals, define specific deadlines or milestones. For example, instead of "Increase sales," specify, "Increase sales by 10% within the next quarter." The defined timeframe motivates the team to stay on track and manage their workload efficiently.

Ask:

When do we want to achieve this goal?

Are there interim milestones to track progress?

What resources are needed to meet the timeline?

Time-bound goals ensure steady progress and create a sense of accomplishment as deadlines are met.

Once SMART goals are in place, regular progress reviews and celebrations of success are essential for maintaining momentum. Periodically evaluate how the team is performing against the goals, and make adjustments as needed. Celebrate milestones, both large and small, to recognize contributions and reinforce motivation.

Schedule regular check-ins to discuss progress, address challenges, and refine strategies. Use these moments to acknowledge achievements, whether it's hitting a milestone, improving efficiency, or overcoming an obstacle. Celebrating progress fosters a positive team culture and reinforces the value of SMART goals as tools for success.

SMART goals turn vision into actionable steps that drive measurable outcomes. By making goals Specific, Measurable, Achievable, Relevant, and Time-bound, you create a clear roadmap that empowers your team to excel. With these goals in place, your team can focus on meaningful work, track their progress, and stay motivated as they bring the vision to life. SMART goals aren't just a framework—they're a tool for building clarity, accountability, and shared success.

Creating Accountability and Tracking Progress

Accountability is the cornerstone of turning ambitions into achievements. When team members feel genuinely responsible for their tasks, they not only stay engaged but also take pride in their contributions. This ownership, paired with effective tracking of progress, transforms goals from abstract concepts into tangible milestones. Leaders who cultivate a culture of accountability and provide clear pathways for tracking success ensure their teams remain aligned, motivated, and purposeful.

Accountability begins with setting the stage for clarity. Each team member must understand their role, the tasks they're responsible for, and how their efforts tie into the team's larger objectives. Defining roles isn't just about delegating tasks; it's about creating a shared understanding of how each piece fits into the puzzle. For example, when a team is tasked with launching a new product, assigning specific responsibilities—such as who oversees market research, who leads design, and who manages outreach—ensures that no effort is redundant or overlooked. This clarity fosters confidence and a natural sense of accountability, as everyone knows what's expected of them and why it matters.

Equally important is having a system for tracking progress. A structured approach to monitoring goals offers insight into what's working, identifies potential roadblocks, and reinforces alignment. Whether through collaborative tools like shared dashboards or regular team check-ins, progress tracking keeps everyone informed and engaged. Imagine a scenario where weekly reviews allow team members to share updates, celebrate wins, and recalibrate timelines when needed. These touchpoints not only reinforce accountability but also promote transparency, as everyone stays aware of how their individual contributions affect the team's collective progress.

Open communication is the lifeblood of accountability. Teams thrive when members feel safe to discuss setbacks, ask for support, and offer feedback without fear of judgment. This openness encourages problem-solving over blame and helps leaders provide timely guidance. When a task isn't progressing as planned, addressing the issue constructively—asking what adjustments might help or what resources are needed—signals a commitment to growth rather than punishment. Leaders who foster this environment demonstrate that accountability isn't about perfection; it's about collaboration and continuous improvement.

Celebrating milestones along the way strengthens the link between accountability and motivation. When achievements, both big and small, are recognized, team members feel valued and energized to continue their efforts. For instance, acknowledging a team's accomplishment in reaching an interim goal, such as completing the first phase of a project on time, reinforces the importance of their work. Celebrations don't have to be extravagant; a heartfelt "thank you" during a meeting or a message of appreciation can create a ripple effect of positivity and momentum.

While staying on course is vital, flexibility in adjusting goals and strategies is equally important. As projects evolve, new information or challenges may surface, requiring a shift in approach. Leaders who embrace adaptability show that accountability is about achieving meaningful results rather than rigidly adhering to a plan. This might mean revising timelines, reallocating resources, or even redefining the scope of a goal. When leaders involve their teams in these adjustments, seeking input and collaboration, they reinforce a sense of shared responsibility and trust.

Ultimately, accountability starts at the top. Leaders who model the behavior they expect—honoring commitments, admitting mistakes, and seeking feedback—set a powerful example. When leaders demonstrate transparency and reliability, they create an environment where accountability feels natural and empowering. By showing that accountability is a shared journey rather than an imposed standard, leaders foster a culture where growth, trust, and excellence thrive.

Tracking progress and maintaining accountability are not isolated actions but continuous practices woven into the fabric of effective teamwork. Through clear expectations, regular feedback, and consistent recognition, leaders can transform accountability into a motivating force. In doing so, they create teams that are not only capable but also deeply committed to achieving success together.

Encouraging Initiative and Autonomy

Empowering your team with initiative and autonomy is one of the most transformative things a leader can do. When people feel trusted to make decisions and take ownership of their work, their creativity and commitment flourish. They approach tasks not as obligations but as opportunities to contribute meaningfully. Initiative drives proactive problem-solving, while autonomy cultivates a sense of personal responsibility that energizes the entire team. Together, these qualities build an environment where individuals feel motivated to excel and empowered to innovate.

Establishing autonomy begins with clarity. People thrive when they understand the goals they're working toward and the boundaries within which they can operate. It's not about giving complete freedom without context—it's about defining the purpose and priorities while allowing flexibility in how the work gets done. For instance, when assigning a project, make the desired outcomes explicit while leaving room for team members to determine the best approach. This balance between structure and freedom encourages independent thought while keeping efforts aligned with the team's vision.

Decision-making is at the heart of autonomy. Trusting team members to make decisions not only demonstrates confidence in their abilities but also cultivates their confidence in themselves. Encourage them to take ownership by assigning responsibilities that match their strengths and aspirations. When they seek guidance, respond with questions that prompt them to think critically, such as, "What do you believe is the best solution, and why?" This approach nurtures decision-making skills and reinforces their ability to act independently.

Autonomy also flourishes in an environment where growth is prioritized. People are more inclined to take initiative when they see opportunities to expand their skills and contribute in new ways. This might involve assigning challenging tasks that push them beyond their comfort zones or supporting their pursuit of learning through workshops and mentorship. Regular feedback further strengthens this dynamic, as it helps team members refine their abilities and remain motivated by the progress they see in themselves.

Innovation thrives when autonomy is paired with creativity. When team members are encouraged to experiment with new approaches, they feel free to explore solutions that go beyond the obvious. Foster this by framing obstacles as opportunities for fresh thinking. A resource limitation, for example, can be presented as a chance to reimagine processes and find efficiencies. Create spaces for brainstorming and open dialogue where every idea is treated with respect and consideration. This trust in their creativity leads to breakthroughs that elevate the team's collective impact.

Of course, autonomy requires trust. Micromanagement stifles initiative and sends the message that decisions must be funneled through the leader. To build a culture of autonomy, focus on outcomes rather than processes. Trust your team to navigate their own paths toward achieving the results you've defined. When mistakes happen, approach them as moments of learning rather than failures, reinforcing that growth often comes from trial and error.

Recognition plays a pivotal role in encouraging initiative. When team members take ownership of their work or solve challenges independently, celebrate these moments. Acknowledge their contributions openly, connecting their efforts to the team's larger goals. This not only boosts morale but also reinforces the value of autonomy, motivating others to follow suit. Recognition should highlight that taking initiative isn't just encouraged—it's a key driver of the team's success.

Ultimately, autonomy and initiative are about fostering a sense of ownership. When team members feel their contributions matter and that they have the freedom to shape outcomes, their engagement deepens. They become invested in not just completing tasks but in making meaningful progress. By cultivating a culture that values independence, supports creativity, and celebrates proactive contributions, leaders create teams that are resilient, innovative, and motivated to excel. This is leadership that inspires—a collective effort where everyone feels empowered to bring their best to the table.

Overcoming Obstacles and Adjusting Goals

Obstacles are an inevitable part of pursuing meaningful goals. They test our resolve, challenge our strategies, and sometimes force us to reconsider how we define success. For leaders, overcoming obstacles isn't just about resolving problems—it's about demonstrating resilience, adaptability, and unwavering focus on the bigger picture. Adjusting goals in response to unforeseen challenges isn't a compromise on ambition; it's a strategic recalibration to keep the team moving forward, united and motivated.

The key to navigating obstacles begins with awareness. Leaders who actively identify potential challenges early create the space to address them constructively. Encouraging open communication within the team is vital. When team members feel safe sharing concerns, they become collaborators in overcoming hurdles rather than passive observers. Instead of allowing obstacles to derail progress, leaders and their teams can approach them proactively, identifying solutions before issues escalate.

Once challenges are recognized, understanding their root causes is essential. Superficial fixes may offer short-term relief but often leave deeper issues unresolved. Leaders must dig deeper, asking the right questions and listening carefully. Is a resource constraint the real issue, or is it a symptom of misaligned priorities? Are delays caused by external factors, or is there an internal bottleneck that needs addressing? By uncovering the true source of the challenge, leaders can craft strategies that address the heart of the problem.

While understanding obstacles is important, shifting the team's mindset is equally critical. A solution-focused approach reframes challenges as opportunities to innovate and grow. When obstacles arise, it's easy to dwell on what's gone wrong. But leaders who redirect their team's energy toward "What can we do next?" foster a culture of optimism and resourcefulness. This mindset isn't about denying the difficulty—it's about choosing to face it with creativity and determination.

Adjusting goals is sometimes necessary, and doing so requires thoughtful leadership. A goal adjustment isn't a defeat; it's a recognition that flexibility is a strength. Whether it's extending a deadline, reallocating resources, or redefining success, leaders who adapt goals while staying true to the team's vision ensure that progress remains meaningful and achievable. Involving the team in this process builds trust and commitment, as it reinforces that their voices matter and that the adjustments serve a shared purpose.

Transparency is essential when goals shift. Communicating clearly about why changes are being made and what they entail helps the team understand the reasoning behind the adjustments. This openness fosters trust and ensures alignment. For example, if a project timeline is extended to accommodate unforeseen delays, explaining the rationale—whether it's to preserve quality, address new opportunities, or reallocate resources—helps the team see the adjustment as a strategic decision rather than a setback.

Motivation can waver during moments of uncertainty, especially when goals evolve. Leaders must work to keep the team inspired by celebrating progress, no matter how incremental. Recognizing milestones reminds everyone of how far they've come and reinforces the value of their efforts. Revisiting the team's overarching vision also grounds their work in purpose, ensuring they remain connected to the "why" even as the "how" evolves.

Perhaps the greatest opportunity that comes from facing obstacles is the chance to learn. Each challenge, regardless of its outcome, provides insights that strengthen the team's resilience. After addressing an obstacle, take time to reflect.

What strategies were most effective? What could have been handled differently?

What did the experience teach about the team's strengths and areas for growth? These lessons become tools for future success, embedding adaptability and improvement into the team's DNA.

Ultimately, obstacles are not roadblocks; they're part of the journey. How a leader responds to them defines the trajectory of the team. By facing challenges with openness, adjusting goals with intention, and maintaining a culture of learning and perseverance, leaders transform setbacks into opportunities for growth. The path to achieving ambitious goals may not always be linear, but with resilience and adaptability, it will always lead forward.

Building A Culture of Continuous Learning and Improvement

Encouraging a Growth Mindset in Your Team

A growth mindset is a transformative force within any team, driving innovation, resilience, and a shared commitment to learning. It shifts the focus from fixed abilities to the boundless potential of development, creating an environment where challenges are welcomed, feedback is valued, and perseverance is celebrated. As a leader, fostering this mindset is not just about encouraging growth in others; it's about embedding the principles of continuous learning into the very fabric of your team's culture.

The most effective way to inspire a growth mindset is to embody it. Your team looks to you as an example, and when they see you openly embrace challenges, acknowledge your own learning journey, and demonstrate humility in the face of mistakes, they will naturally feel encouraged to do the same. Transparency about your development not only humanizes you as a leader but also underscores that growth is a universal pursuit. For example, admitting, "I learned a lot from this decision, and here's how I'm applying it moving forward," communicates that progress stems from effort, reflection, and the willingness to evolve.

Challenges become fertile ground for growth when reframed as opportunities. As a leader, your role is to guide the narrative around obstacles, transforming them from burdens to learning experiences. When faced with a setback, your perspective shapes the team's response. Rather than framing it as a failure, position it as a valuable step in the journey. For instance, encountering an unexpected roadblock in a project could become an opportunity to explore alternative solutions, develop new skills, or strengthen collaboration. Posing reflective questions like, "What can we learn from this?" or "How can we leverage this experience to improve?" keeps the focus on discovery and progress.

Constructive feedback is another cornerstone of fostering a growth mindset. Feedback should never feel like criticism; instead, it should be an invitation to grow. Specificity is key—address behaviors and strategies rather than intrinsic qualities. Consider how you would approach a team member who struggled to meet a deadline. Instead of saying, "You're not good with time management," you might suggest, "Let's explore ways to prioritize tasks more effectively to meet deadlines in the future." This approach reinforces the belief that skills can be developed, guiding the team member toward actionable steps for improvement.

Effort, not perfection, should be the marker of success in a growth-oriented culture. When leaders celebrate the dedication and progress that lead to outcomes, they reinforce the value of persistence and learning. Recognizing effort might look like applauding a team member who tackled a challenging task for the first time or commending the team for innovative thinking, even if the results weren't flawless. Highlighting the process instills confidence, encouraging team members to continue pushing boundaries and embracing the unknown.

A culture of growth thrives on the foundation of lifelong learning. By offering opportunities for development—whether through formal training, cross-functional projects, or mentorship—you signal that growth is an ongoing priority. Equally important is fostering a space for peer-to-peer learning, where insights and skills are shared openly. These moments of collaboration not only enhance collective knowledge but also strengthen bonds within the team, building a sense of shared purpose.

Mistakes, often seen as setbacks, are invaluable teachers. Normalizing mistakes as part of the learning process liberates your team from the fear of failure, fostering a willingness to experiment and innovate. When mistakes happen, approach them with curiosity rather than judgment. For instance, after a misstep in a presentation, you might ask, "What could we do differently next time?" or "What did this experience teach us about our approach?" This reframing creates psychological safety, empowering team members to take calculated risks and learn without fear of reprimand.

By fostering a growth mindset, you cultivate a team that thrives on curiosity, adaptability, and resilience. It's a mindset that doesn't just prepare your team for challenges—it transforms those challenges into stepping stones for achievement. Together, you'll not only reach new heights but also redefine what's possible, united by a shared belief in the power of effort, learning, and growth.

Establishing a Continuous Feedback Loop

Creating a continuous feedback loop within your team is like constructing a bridge between potential and progress—a dynamic process that not only guides individual growth but also strengthens the team as a whole. Feedback is most effective when it's not a sporadic event but an ongoing dialogue that informs, inspires, and motivates. By making feedback a regular, structured part of your leadership approach, you establish a foundation of trust, accountability, and development that empowers your team to thrive.

At the heart of this process lies trust. Without trust, feedback can feel like criticism or judgment, but with trust, it becomes a valuable tool for growth. As a leader, building this trust starts with creating an atmosphere where feedback is welcomed and expected. Begin by normalizing feedback as a two-way street—something that flows not only from leader to team member but also in the opposite direction. When you openly invite feedback on your leadership style or decision-making, you demonstrate humility and a commitment to improvement. For instance, simply asking, "How can I better support you in achieving your goals?" can open the door to meaningful dialogue. This approach shows your team that feedback isn't about fault-finding; it's about fostering mutual success.

Timeliness and specificity are essential for making feedback impactful. Feedback given in the moment—or as close to it as possible—carries more weight because it connects directly to actions or events that are fresh in memory. Imagine a team member has just delivered a presentation. Waiting weeks to provide feedback dilutes its relevance, but offering immediate, thoughtful insights reinforces their strengths and highlights areas for improvement while the experience is still vivid. Specificity amplifies this impact. Vague comments like "Good job" or "You need to improve" lack the detail needed for actionable change. Instead, you might say, "Your visuals were compelling and really engaged the audience. Next time, consider slowing down during key points to ensure your message lands effectively." This kind of targeted feedback gives clear direction while reinforcing positive behaviors.

A continuous feedback loop is as much about listening as it is about giving advice. Encouraging team members to assess their own performance fosters self-awareness and empowers them to take ownership of their development. Before feedback sessions, prompt reflection with questions like, "What do you think went well in this project?" or "What challenges did you face, and how did you address them?" When team members come prepared with their own insights, the conversation becomes a collaborative exploration rather than a one-sided critique. Listening actively to their reflections also provides you with valuable context, deepening your understanding of their motivations and needs.

Regular, structured check-ins are the scaffolding of an effective feedback loop. Whether weekly, bi-weekly, or monthly, these sessions create a rhythm of communication that keeps growth at the forefront. A one-on-one meeting might focus on immediate tasks or short-term goals, while quarterly reviews could delve into long-term aspirations and skill development. Each session is an opportunity to reinforce progress, address challenges, and realign efforts with team objectives. By making these conversations consistent, you signal to your team that their growth is a priority.

Celebrating achievements—no matter how small—injects positivity into the feedback loop and keeps team members motivated. Recognizing effort and progress shows that you value the journey as much as the destination. If a team member has been working on improving their collaboration skills, acknowledge their strides: "I've noticed how you've been actively engaging with others during brainstorming sessions, and it's really helping elevate the team's creativity." This kind of reinforcement not only boosts morale but also reinforces the behaviors you want to see more of.

Feedback is most effective when it's paired with clear, actionable goals. Use insights from your conversations to co-create development objectives that are specific, measurable, and time-bound. For example, if a team member is looking to enhance their project management skills, set a goal like, "Lead the next team initiative from start to finish, ensuring all milestones are met within the next three months." Goals like this provide a roadmap for improvement and a sense of purpose, transforming feedback into tangible progress.

Adapting to feedback and adjusting goals as needed is a sign of a healthy, thriving team. Not every plan will go smoothly, and not every goal will be met as expected. That's why a feedback loop needs to be flexible. When obstacles arise, revisit goals with your team and collaboratively identify adjustments. This adaptability not only keeps momentum alive but also reinforces the idea that growth is a dynamic, evolving process.

By weaving continuous feedback into the fabric of your leadership, you create a culture where learning and improvement are constant, celebrated, and shared. Your team becomes more engaged, more resilient, and more aligned with their goals and the organization's vision. Ultimately, a continuous feedback loop is not just about refining skills— it's about building a team that thrives on growth, values collaboration, and pursues excellence with confidence and purpose.

Promoting Knowledge Sharing and Collaboration

Promoting knowledge sharing and collaboration within your team is like planting seeds in fertile soil—it lays the groundwork for collective growth, creativity, and adaptability. When people share ideas, skills, and experiences openly, they enrich one another's perspectives and strengthen the team's ability to innovate and solve complex problems. As a leader, your role is to cultivate this environment by fostering trust, encouraging dialogue, and celebrating contributions.

At the core of a collaborative team is open communication. This is where knowledge sharing begins. When team members feel comfortable voicing their ideas and asking questions, it creates a natural flow of information. To encourage this openness, lead by example. Share your own insights, whether they're lessons learned from a recent project, observations about industry trends, or strategies you've seen work in other contexts. Transparency from you sets the tone for the entire team, showing that no contribution is too small and that knowledge is meant to be shared, not hoarded.

Creating dedicated spaces for idea exchange further supports this dynamic. Regular team meetings, brainstorming sessions, or informal coffee chats can serve as platforms where everyone feels encouraged to contribute. Imagine the power of starting a meeting by asking, "What's one thing you've learned this week that could help the team?" It's simple, yet it sparks a mindset of curiosity and collective learning. Over time, these practices build trust and make sharing second nature.

Mentorship and peer learning amplify the impact of knowledge sharing. Think of mentorship as a bridge between experience and potential. Pairing team members who excel in certain areas with those eager to grow creates a mutual exchange. For the mentor, it's an opportunity to refine their skills and leadership. For the mentee, it's a chance to learn directly from a trusted guide. And peer learning doesn't have to be formal. Something as casual as a "lunch-and-learn" session, where team members take turns presenting on topics they're passionate about, can foster connection and spark fresh ideas.

Technology is another powerful ally. Digital tools like shared drives, project management platforms, or collaborative apps make it easy to capture and share knowledge. A shared repository, for example, can act as a living library of resources— guides, templates, or research—that everyone can access and contribute to. But technology isn't just about convenience; it's about breaking down barriers. With tools like Slack or Microsoft Teams, collaboration happens in real-time, whether your team is in the same office or spread across continents. Encourage your team to use these platforms actively, not just for updates but to share insights, ask for advice, or celebrate wins.

Recognition is the glue that holds a knowledge-sharing culture together. When someone takes the time to teach, mentor, or contribute an idea, their effort deserves to be acknowledged. Recognition doesn't have to be grand—sometimes, a simple "Thank you for sharing that perspective; it really shaped our approach" can make all the difference. If you want to formalize it, consider creating a tradition, like a monthly "Knowledge Champion" award, to celebrate those who go above and beyond in fostering collaboration.

Collaboration reaches new heights when it extends beyond the immediate team. Cross-functional projects are an excellent way to do this, exposing your team to new expertise and ways of thinking. For example, if your team is working on a new product, involve members from marketing, operations, or even customer service. These interactions not only enrich the project but also create networks of knowledge that your team can draw from in the future. Workshops or panel discussions featuring colleagues from other departments can also be a great way to encourage cross-functional learning.

Ultimately, fostering a culture of collaboration hinges on instilling a mindset of continuous improvement. It's about creating an environment where team members don't just ask, "What can I contribute?" but also, "What can I learn?" Encourage this by normalizing questions and celebrating curiosity. As a leader, share your learning journey—talk about books you're reading, courses you're taking, or lessons you've picked up along the way. When you model this mindset, it signals to your team that growth is a shared value.

When knowledge flows freely and collaboration thrives, the possibilities are endless. Your team becomes more resilient, adaptable, and innovative, ready to tackle challenges with a sense of shared purpose. By creating an environment where ideas are exchanged openly and learning is celebrated, you're not just building a team—you're cultivating a community where everyone has the opportunity to grow and succeed together.

Supporting Professional Development and Growth

Supporting professional development within a team is like watering the roots of a thriving plant—focused attention and care allow growth that benefits not only individuals but the entire ecosystem. When leaders prioritize professional development, they create an environment where curiosity, growth, and purpose flourish. The result? Team members who feel valued, equipped, and motivated to excel in their roles and contribute meaningfully to collective goals.

The first step in fostering professional growth is understanding what each team member aspires to achieve. This isn't about a one-size-fits-all approach. Each person brings a unique set of talents, experiences, and ambitions. When you take the time to have genuine conversations about their goals, you signal that their growth matters. Ask thoughtful, open-ended questions like, "What challenges excite you?" or "What skills do you see as crucial for your next step?" These discussions lay the groundwork for development plans that are as individualized as they are actionable.

But talking about growth is just the beginning. Development thrives on opportunities—and providing access to them is where leaders truly make an impact. Whether it's encouraging attendance at a leadership seminar, offering mentorship within the team, or assigning stretch projects that challenge comfort zones, these opportunities transform aspirations into action. Imagine a team member who wants to build leadership skills. Assigning them to spearhead a project not only sharpens their abilities but also demonstrates trust in their potential.

At the same time, learning doesn't always have to happen in structured settings. Supporting informal, self-paced exploration—like diving into an online course or reading industry-related books—cultivates a love for lifelong learning. Leaders who promote this kind of self-direction empower their team to take ownership of their growth, creating a ripple effect of curiosity and initiative.

To make development tangible, structured plans and progress tracking are invaluable. Development plans act as roadmaps, detailing where someone is going and how they'll get there. These plans should include clear milestones and regular check-ins to celebrate progress or recalibrate when necessary. This isn't about micromanaging; it's about fostering accountability and giving team members a sense of momentum as they advance toward their goals.

Yet, professional development is never just an individual journey—it's intrinsically tied to the team's collective success. Growth that aligns with the team's objectives amplifies impact. When a team member learns a new skill or gains fresh insight, the ripple effects can drive innovation, solve complex challenges, or improve workflows. Leaders who make these connections clear inspire team members to grow not just for their benefit but for the good of the team as a whole.

Recognition plays a pivotal role in sustaining the energy and enthusiasm for growth. Celebrate when someone earns a certification, masters a new skill, or applies a learning breakthrough to a project. Whether it's a public acknowledgment during a team meeting or a personal note of thanks, these gestures reinforce that effort and progress matter.

Lastly, growth requires a foundation of support. Leaders must create an environment where experimenting and even failing are safe. When someone stumbles while trying to apply a new skill, offer guidance instead of critique. Ask, "What did you learn?" and "How can we adjust to try again?" These moments of support foster resilience and demonstrate that professional development is a journey, not a race to perfection.

Investing in professional development is about building more than skills; it's about building people. When leaders commit to nurturing growth, they inspire their team to aim higher, dig deeper, and bring their best to the table every day. The ultimate reward? A dynamic, forward-thinking team that's equipped to meet today's challenges and embrace tomorrow's opportunities.

Celebrating Achievements and Learning from Challenges

Celebrating achievements and learning from challenges are the dual engines that drive a high-performing team. Successes fuel motivation and reinforce positive behaviors, while challenges teach resilience, adaptability, and problem-solving. Together, they create a balanced, growth-oriented culture where team members feel valued for their contributions and inspired to continuously improve.

Celebrating achievements, whether they are monumental victories or small daily wins, builds momentum and morale. It's not just about recognizing outcomes—it's about acknowledging the effort, collaboration, and creativity that make those outcomes possible. A simple, heartfelt acknowledgment like, "Your dedication to this project ensured its success. Well done!" can make a lasting impact. For team-wide milestones, celebrations that involve everyone—such as a shared lunch or a public shout-out—remind individuals that their contributions matter to the collective success.

Reflection turns success into a learning opportunity. After celebrating, ask, "What made this achievement possible?" and "How can we replicate this success in the future?" These reflections crystallize effective strategies and reinforce the behaviors that drive results. By taking a moment to learn from victories, the team gains a deeper understanding of what works, ensuring that success isn't just a one-time event but a repeatable process.

Challenges, on the other hand, offer a different kind of value. They are the crucibles where growth happens, testing the team's creativity, resilience, and resolve. Leaders play a crucial role in normalizing challenges, framing them not as failures but as opportunities to learn and improve. When obstacles arise, lead with questions like, "What can we learn from this?" or "How can we adapt our approach?" This mindset shift transforms setbacks into stepping stones.

Reflection on challenges should be constructive and forward-looking. Create a safe space for candid discussions about what went wrong, why, and how the team can do better next time. Avoid focusing on blame and instead emphasize growth. For instance, if a project faced delays due to miscommunication, frame it as, "This gives us an opportunity to refine our communication processes for future projects."

Equally important is balancing celebration and reflection, especially in the face of adversity. Even during challenging times, acknowledge the effort and perseverance that the team demonstrated. A comment like, "I know this didn't go as planned, but I'm proud of how we tackled the problem together," validates their hard work while setting a constructive tone for reflection. This balance ensures that setbacks don't demoralize the team but instead energize them for the next challenge.

Leaders who consistently celebrate achievements and learn from challenges reinforce a culture of resilience and growth.

They remind the team that every experience—whether triumphant or tough—contributes to the bigger picture of progress and success. This dual focus on celebrating and learning prepares the team to face the future with confidence, creativity, and a relentless drive to improve.

Leading Through Change and Uncertainty

Understanding the Dynamics of Change

Understanding the dynamics of change is essential for leaders navigating transitions. Change, whether big or small, can significantly impact team morale, productivity, and cohesion. It often evokes a spectrum of emotions—uncertainty, fear, resistance, but also hope and excitement. Leaders who grasp these dynamics can transform change from a source of anxiety into a powerful opportunity for growth and innovation.

At the heart of effective change management lies the ability to recognize its stages. Team members may initially react with shock or resistance as they grapple with the implications. Acknowledging these emotions isn't just compassionate; it's strategic. For example, when introducing a new system, a leader might say, "I understand this shift feels daunting, but it's a step toward simplifying our work in the long run." This recognition sets the tone for openness and trust.

As the team moves past initial resistance, they may start exploring possibilities within the new framework. This exploration stage is where leaders can nurture curiosity and optimism by framing the change as a learning opportunity. Statements like, "This new system allows us to streamline tasks and focus on creative solutions," help anchor the change in tangible benefits. Encouraging questions and facilitating hands-on learning sessions also build confidence and competence.

Clear communication about the "why" behind the change is another cornerstone of managing transitions effectively. People resist change more when it feels arbitrary or disconnected from their goals. Leaders who connect the dots between the change and the team's shared mission foster alignment and buy-in. For instance, explaining that a restructuring will better position the team to innovate shows how short-term adjustments lead to long-term benefits.

Providing resources and continuous support ensures that your team isn't just adapting—they're thriving. Change often requires skill-building or mindset shifts. Leaders can set the stage by offering access to tools, training, or mentorship. For example, if a new digital tool is being adopted, providing tutorials, scheduling practice sessions, and making experts available for questions can turn a source of stress into a growth opportunity. Regular check-ins during these transitions show your investment in their success.

Beyond logistics, fostering a culture of adaptability and resilience prepares teams to weather future changes. When leaders model a positive attitude toward change, they set the tone for their teams. Sharing personal stories about times when adaptability led to unexpected success can be a powerful motivator. Celebrating moments of resilience—whether it's a team member mastering a new skill or collaborating in innovative ways—reinforces that change isn't just something to survive but an opportunity to thrive.

Ultimately, leaders who approach change with empathy and strategy empower their teams to view it as a catalyst for progress. By balancing the acknowledgment of challenges with a focus on possibilities, you create an environment where change becomes a shared journey toward improvement. With this mindset, even the most daunting transitions can strengthen the team's cohesion, resilience, and drive for excellence.

Communicating Effectively During Change

Communicating effectively during change is the cornerstone of navigating transitions successfully. Change, while inevitable, can often stir uncertainty and resistance within a team. Leaders who approach communication with clarity, consistency, and empathy pave the way for smoother transitions, ensuring their team feels informed, supported, and motivated to move forward.

At the heart of effective change communication is a clear and compelling vision. Articulating why the change is happening and how it aligns with the organization's mission connects the transition to a greater purpose. For instance, a leader might explain, "We're implementing this new system to improve efficiency and allow us to focus more on creative solutions for our clients." Framing the change within the context of shared goals not only provides clarity but also fosters a sense of shared commitment.

Transparency plays an equally critical role. When leaders are upfront about both the benefits and challenges of a change, they cultivate trust. Acknowledging uncertainties, such as, "We understand this adjustment may feel overwhelming at first, but we're committed to providing the training and support needed," reassures team members that their concerns are recognized and will be addressed.

Consistent updates are vital in maintaining momentum and clarity. Leaders should create a cadence of communication—whether through emails, team huddles, or one-on-one discussions—that keeps everyone informed. For example, providing regular progress reports on the rollout of a new initiative helps team members feel connected to the process, even if they're not directly involved in every phase. Reiterating key messages ensures that the purpose and benefits of the change remain top of mind.

Equally important is fostering dialogue. Change is not just about broadcasting information; it's about listening. Leaders should create spaces where team members can ask questions, voice concerns, and share ideas. Open forums, anonymous feedback channels, or informal coffee chats can be instrumental in making team members feel heard. A leader who listens actively and responds thoughtfully—acknowledging even concerns that can't be resolved immediately—strengthens the team's trust and buy-in.

Empathy anchors all effective change communication. Recognizing the emotional impact of change validates team members' experiences and builds a supportive environment. Simple yet intentional language, like "I know this transition brings new challenges, and it's okay to feel uncertain. Let's work together to navigate this," goes a long way in fostering confidence and resilience.

Celebrating milestones during a change process is often overlooked but deeply impactful. Acknowledging achievements, no matter how small, reinforces the team's progress and adaptability. Whether it's completing a training session or reaching a key project milestone, celebrating these wins instills a sense of accomplishment and motivates the team to keep pushing forward.

Effective communication during change is not just about delivering information; it's about fostering connection, trust, and a shared sense of purpose. By crafting a clear vision, maintaining transparency, inviting dialogue, and showing empathy, leaders create an environment where change feels less like a disruption and more like an opportunity. With these strategies, leaders empower their teams to navigate uncertainty with confidence, emerging stronger and more united on the other side.

Supporting Team Morale and Motivation Through Change

Change can bring challenges and uncertainty that impact team morale and motivation. When routines are disrupted, roles are adjusted, or responsibilities shift, it's natural for team members to feel unsettled. Leaders who focus on maintaining morale and fostering motivation provide a stabilizing influence, helping the team stay positive, engaged, and focused on shared goals. By actively supporting well-being and celebrating progress, leaders create an atmosphere of encouragement and resilience, empowering team members to approach change with confidence and enthusiasm.

Supporting morale during change requires a combination of empathy, recognition, and communication. When team members feel appreciated, supported, and connected to a shared purpose, they're more likely to navigate transitions successfully, remaining committed to their roles and motivated to contribute to the team's success.

Emotional support is crucial for sustaining morale during times of change. Leaders who offer empathy, reassurance, and a listening ear create a safe space where team members can express their concerns and find comfort in knowing they're not alone. By addressing emotional needs, you help the team feel more grounded, reducing stress and fostering a sense of stability.

To provide emotional support, acknowledge the impact of the change and validate each person's feelings. Let team members know that it's natural to feel uncertain or anxious and that their concerns are understood. For example, you might say, "I understand that this change might feel overwhelming, and I want you to know that I'm here to support you every step of the way." This reassurance creates a supportive atmosphere, where team members feel respected and valued.

Encourage open conversations about the emotional impact of the change. Invite team members to share their thoughts and feelings, and listen actively, responding with empathy and understanding. This open dialogue not only reinforces morale but also strengthens trust, as team members see that their leader genuinely cares about their well-being.

Flexibility and adaptability are essential for maintaining morale during change, as they empower team members to adjust without feeling overwhelmed. Leaders who encourage flexibility provide team members with the freedom to explore new approaches, set their own pace, and adjust as needed, making the transition process more manageable and less daunting.

Promote flexibility by adjusting expectations as the team adapts to new roles, responsibilities, or workflows. Recognize that there may be a learning curve, and reassure team members that it's okay to take time to adjust. For example, you might say, "Feel free to experiment with different methods as you get used to this new system. We'll work together to find what works best." This adaptability creates a sense of empowerment, as team members feel trusted to navigate the change in ways that suit their individual needs.

Additionally, encourage team members to support one another's efforts to adapt. Promote a collaborative atmosphere where team members can share insights, offer feedback, and discuss ways to adjust effectively. This culture of adaptability reinforces resilience, as everyone feels empowered to approach change with creativity and an open mind.

During change, maintaining a sense of purpose and connection to shared goals is essential for sustaining motivation. Leaders who remind the team of their collective mission help members see the value of their work, even as circumstances shift.

A clear purpose reinforces morale, as team members feel connected to something meaningful and see that their contributions still matter.

To reinforce a sense of purpose, remind the team of the organization's vision and how the change supports long-term goals. Explain how their work, efforts, and dedication contribute to the team's success, even as roles or responsibilities evolve. For instance, if the change involves implementing a new strategy, emphasize how each team member's contributions will help achieve positive results, such as improved customer satisfaction or streamlined operations.

Encourage team members to reflect on their individual impact by asking questions like, "How does your role contribute to our team's success?" or "What positive impact can we create together through this transition?" This focus on purpose keeps team members motivated, as they see that their efforts are valuable and aligned with meaningful goals.

Celebrating small wins and acknowledging progress is a powerful way to boost morale and sustain motivation during change. Leaders who recognize milestones, big or small, provide positive reinforcement that makes the transition feel more rewarding. Celebrations also create a sense of momentum, as team members see tangible evidence of their progress, reinforcing their confidence and commitment.

Identify specific milestones within the change process, whether it's mastering a new skill, completing a phase of a project, or reaching a performance target. Celebrate each milestone openly, acknowledging the team's hard work and perseverance. For example, if the team successfully completes a training session, you might say, "Thank you for your commitment to learning this new tool. Your hard work is helping us make great strides, and I'm proud of the progress we're making together."

In addition to group celebrations, acknowledge individual achievements that contribute to the team's success. Recognize team members who show resilience, offer support to others, or adapt creatively, reinforcing the value of their contributions. By celebrating both individual and collective progress, you keep morale high, inspiring team members to stay engaged and motivated.

Change can bring additional stress, and leaders who encourage self-care and work-life balance help team members manage their well-being during transitions. By supporting healthy boundaries and encouraging self-care practices, you create a balanced environment where team members feel valued and supported both personally and professionally.

Encourage team members to prioritize self-care, whether through breaks, exercise, or time spent with family and friends. Remind them that taking care of their well-being enhances their ability to adapt, stay focused, and contribute effectively. For instance, you might say, "As we navigate this change, remember to prioritize your well-being. Taking time to recharge will help us all stay resilient and focused." This reminder reinforces the importance of balance, making it clear that their health and happiness are essential to the team's success.

Additionally, promote work-life balance by setting reasonable expectations, respecting boundaries, and modeling healthy habits yourself. When team members see that you value balance, they feel empowered to manage their own well-being, making it easier to stay motivated and focused.

Creating a supportive, encouraging team culture helps maintain morale during change, as team members feel connected to one another and motivated to succeed together. Leaders who foster mutual support create an environment where everyone feels valued, heard, and empowered to offer help, strengthening resilience and collaboration.

Encourage team members to share their experiences, insights, and strategies for adapting to the change. Create opportunities for peer support, whether through small group discussions, mentoring pairs, or collaborative projects. Emphasize that everyone has valuable perspectives and experiences to contribute, making it clear that they're all in this transition together.

Celebrate acts of encouragement, such as team members who help each other learn new skills, offer words of support, or show empathy during difficult moments. Acknowledge these actions openly, reinforcing a culture where mutual support is valued and appreciated. By promoting encouragement and collaboration, you build a team that's not only capable of adapting to change but also inspired to thrive together.

Supporting team morale and motivation through change creates a positive, resilient environment where team members feel appreciated, empowered, and connected to their purpose. By providing emotional support, promoting flexibility, reinforcing purpose, celebrating progress, encouraging self-care, and fostering a culture of encouragement, leaders guide their team through transitions with confidence and optimism. In this supportive atmosphere, team members are better prepared to face challenges, adapt to new circumstances, and continue contributing to the team's success.

Building Trust and Transparency During Transitions

Trust and transparency are essential elements of effective leadership, especially during times of change. Leaders who communicate openly, act with integrity, and follow through on commitments create an environment where team members feel secure, valued, and aligned with the transition's goals. Trust gives team members confidence in their leader's decisions and direction, while transparency reduces anxiety, as people feel informed and prepared to face new challenges. Together, trust and transparency foster a culture of resilience, where team members are empowered to navigate transitions with confidence.

Building trust and transparency requires consistent, honest communication, a willingness to address concerns, and a commitment to keeping the team informed. When team members see that their leader is both reliable and forthcoming, they're more likely to approach change with optimism and a sense of shared purpose, strengthening their engagement and commitment.

Open, consistent communication is the foundation of transparency. Leaders who communicate regularly with their team during transitions provide clarity and reduce uncertainty, ensuring that everyone understands the change's purpose, progress, and impact. By keeping the lines of communication open, you create a culture where team members feel informed and valued, making it easier for them to stay engaged and focused on their goals.

Establish a communication schedule that includes regular updates, team meetings, and one-on-one check-ins. Use these sessions to share information about the transition, answer questions, and reinforce key messages. For instance, if the change involves a new strategy, hold weekly updates to discuss progress, address any adjustments, and outline the next steps. This consistent communication helps team members feel included in the process, reinforcing trust and engagement.

When providing updates, be clear and specific about what's changing, why it matters, and how it affects the team. Use direct language to avoid ambiguity, making it easier for team members to understand the details. By being transparent about the change, you reduce uncertainty, helping team members feel more secure and prepared.

Reliability is a key component of trust. Leaders who follow

through on their commitments demonstrate that they are dependable, reinforcing the team's confidence in their leadership. When team members see that their leader consistently meets promises and expectations, they're more likely to trust that future decisions and directions will be made with integrity and responsibility.

To build reliability, be mindful of the commitments you make and ensure that you can follow through. Set realistic expectations, whether it's about providing support, addressing challenges, or delivering updates. For example, if you commit to checking in weekly during the transition, honor that commitment consistently, showing that your promises are more than just words.

When circumstances make it difficult to meet a commitment, communicate openly and transparently about the reasons. Explain any delays or changes, and provide an updated plan, showing that you're accountable to the team. By maintaining this level of integrity, you reinforce trust, showing that you're dedicated to supporting the team and guiding them through the change.

Leaders who acknowledge uncertainties and address concerns create an environment where team members feel respected and supported. During change, not every question may have an immediate answer, and leaders who are honest about this reinforce a culture of transparency. By addressing uncertainties openly, you build credibility, showing that you're committed to finding solutions and providing guidance.

When team members express concerns or uncertainties, listen actively and respond with empathy. Acknowledge that the change may bring unknowns and that it's normal to feel uncertain. For example, you might say, "I understand that there are still unanswered questions, and I want you to know that we're actively working on solutions. I'll keep you updated as we make progress." This approach reinforces trust, as team members see that you're not dismissing their concerns but rather addressing them with understanding and commitment.

If there are areas where specific answers aren't yet available, be honest about this. Let the team know that you're working to find clarity and that you'll share updates as soon as more information is available. This transparency reduces speculation and keeps the team focused on what they can control, rather than on unknowns.

Trust grows in an environment where team members feel comfortable expressing their thoughts, asking questions, and providing feedback. Leaders who encourage open dialogue create a culture where everyone's perspectives are valued, making it easier for team members to address concerns constructively. By fostering open feedback, you show that you're committed to supporting the team's needs and creating a collaborative atmosphere.

Invite team members to share their thoughts and questions regularly, whether in team meetings, anonymous feedback channels, or one-on-one sessions. Let them know that their feedback is valued and that it plays an important role in shaping the transition process. For instance, you might say, "I encourage you to share any concerns or ideas. Your feedback helps us make this transition as smooth and successful as possible."

Respond to feedback openly, showing appreciation for team members' input. Even if specific suggestions can't be implemented, acknowledge them and explain your reasoning, demonstrating that you value each contribution. By encouraging open feedback and responding thoughtfully, you reinforce transparency and trust, as team members see that their voices are heard and respected.

Integrity is at the heart of trust. Leaders who model honesty and integrity set a standard that inspires team members to approach change with authenticity and accountability. By demonstrating a commitment to truthfulness and ethical decision-making, you create a culture where team members feel secure and confident in your leadership.

Model integrity by being transparent about both successes and challenges. Share not only the positive aspects of the transition but also any difficulties or setbacks the team may encounter. This balanced approach builds trust, as team members see that you're committed to providing accurate information, even when it involves acknowledging obstacles.

Additionally, demonstrate ethical decision-making by considering the team's best interests and acting in ways that reflect the organization's values. For example, if a change involves budget adjustments, explain how decisions were made with fairness and long-term success in mind. By showing that you prioritize integrity, you reinforce the team's confidence in your leadership, making it easier for them to approach the transition with trust and dedication.

Recognizing and celebrating transparency within the team reinforces the value of open communication and trust. When team members see that honesty is appreciated, they're more likely to approach the transition with openness, feeling empowered to share their thoughts, address challenges, and collaborate effectively.

Acknowledge team members who demonstrate transparency, whether by sharing insights, voicing concerns, or supporting colleagues through the transition. For example, you might say, "Thank you for being open about the challenges you're facing with this new system. Your honesty helps us address issues as a team, making the transition smoother for everyone." This recognition reinforces a culture where transparency is valued, encouraging everyone to approach the change with authenticity and collaboration.

Consider establishing transparency as a team value, emphasizing its importance in communication, problem-solving, and relationship-building. By celebrating transparency and honesty, you build a team culture where trust is prioritized, making it easier for everyone to navigate change together with integrity and mutual support.

Building trust and transparency during transitions creates a resilient, supportive environment where team members feel valued, informed, and motivated to adapt. By communicating openly, following through on commitments, acknowledging uncertainties, encouraging dialogue, modeling integrity, and celebrating transparency, leaders reinforce a foundation of trust that empowers the team to navigate change confidently. With trust and transparency as guiding principles, your team is better prepared to embrace challenges, stay engaged, and contribute meaningfully to the shared vision.

Strengthening Team Resilience for Future Changes

Resilience is the ability to adapt to change, overcome challenges, and remain focused on goals despite setbacks. Teams with strong resilience are better equipped to navigate transitions, stay motivated through uncertainty, and embrace new opportunities with optimism. Leaders who prioritize resilience help their team develop the skills, mindsets, and support systems needed to handle both current and future changes successfully. By fostering resilience, you create a culture of strength and adaptability, where team members feel confident in their capacity to face challenges and remain engaged in their work.

Building resilience within a team requires a proactive approach that includes developing skills, encouraging a positive outlook, and reinforcing support networks. With these foundations, your team is prepared not only to survive change but to thrive, growing stronger and more capable with each new challenge.

A growth mindset—the belief that abilities can be developed through dedication and effort—is essential for resilience. Leaders who encourage a growth mindset help their team view challenges as opportunities for learning and improvement, making it easier for them to stay motivated and adaptable during change. By promoting positivity and a focus on personal growth, you empower team members to approach uncertainty with curiosity and resilience.

To foster a growth mindset, model it in your own approach to change. Demonstrate optimism and a willingness to learn, even when facing difficult transitions. For example, if a new process is being introduced, express enthusiasm for the chance to improve efficiency or develop new skills, saying something like, "This change gives us an opportunity to grow and strengthen our capabilities as a team."

Encourage team members to adopt this mindset by celebrating effort, persistence, and learning. Recognize their willingness to try new things, embrace challenges, or develop new skills. By valuing growth over perfection, you create a culture where team members feel safe to experiment, learn from setbacks, and remain resilient through any change.

Adaptability is a core component of resilience, enabling team members to adjust their approach and skills to meet evolving demands. Leaders who prioritize skill-building give their team the tools they need to remain effective and engaged, no matter what changes arise. By investing in skill development, you empower team members to approach future challenges with confidence, knowing they're equipped to handle new tasks, roles, or responsibilities.

Identify skills that enhance adaptability, such as problem-solving, critical thinking, and effective communication. Offer opportunities for team members to develop these skills, whether through training sessions, workshops, or on-the-job experiences. For instance, if the team will be adopting a new project management system, provide hands-on training that allows team members to practice using the system before it's fully implemented. This skill-building reinforces their ability to adapt, reducing anxiety and boosting resilience.

Encourage team members to take ownership of their development by setting personal goals and exploring new learning opportunities. When team members feel empowered to grow, they become more adaptable, as they see each change as a chance to strengthen their skill set and increase their value to the team.

A supportive network is crucial for resilience, as it provides team members with the encouragement, guidance, and resources they need to stay motivated during change. Leaders who foster a sense of community create a safety net where team members feel valued and supported, making it easier for them to handle challenges together. By building a strong support network, you reinforce the team's collective resilience, ensuring that everyone has a reliable source of encouragement during difficult transitions.

Encourage team members to support each other by creating opportunities for collaboration, knowledge sharing, and peer mentorship. For instance, pair team members with complementary skills on projects, allowing them to learn from each other and develop a sense of camaraderie. Additionally, establish regular check-ins where team members can share insights, ask for advice, or offer encouragement. These interactions strengthen the team's bonds, creating a culture of mutual support.

As a leader, model supportive behavior by offering encouragement, recognizing each team member's strengths, and being available for guidance. This approach reinforces the importance of collaboration and makes it clear that resilience is a shared responsibility, where everyone contributes to the team's success.

Self-care is essential for resilience, as it helps team members manage stress, recharge, and maintain motivation during change.

Leaders who encourage work-life balance create an environment where team members feel supported in taking care of their well-being, making it easier for them to stay resilient, focused, and engaged. By promoting self-care, you reinforce the idea that resilience requires both mental and physical well-being.

Encourage team members to prioritize self-care by setting healthy boundaries and managing their workload effectively. Remind them of the importance of breaks, exercise, and time spent away from work, especially during periods of change. For example, you might say, "It's important to take time to recharge. Balancing work with rest helps us stay strong and focused, even as we navigate new challenges."

Additionally, model self-care by managing your own workload, taking breaks, and setting boundaries. When team members see that you value balance, they feel empowered to do the same, making it easier for them to maintain their resilience and well-being.

Embedding resilience as a core team value creates a culture where adaptability, persistence, and optimism are prioritized. Leaders who reinforce resilience as a shared value help team members see its importance in their roles, making it a natural part of their approach to work and change. By celebrating resilience and recognizing efforts to adapt, you create a culture where each team member feels empowered to embrace challenges and continue growing.

Highlight resilience as a team value by discussing it openly in meetings, setting goals that reinforce adaptability, and celebrating examples of resilience in action. For example, if a team member takes on a new role or responsibility during a transition, recognize their willingness to adapt, saying something like, "Your flexibility and positive attitude have made a real difference as we navigate this change. Thank you for your resilience." This recognition reinforces resilience as a valued trait, encouraging others to approach change with the same mindset.

Consider setting team goals that focus on resilience, such as learning new skills, developing problem-solving strategies, or supporting each other during challenging times. By making resilience a priority, you create a culture where team members feel motivated to grow and adapt continuously, confident in their ability to handle any changes that come their way.

Strengthening team resilience for future changes builds a foundation of adaptability, optimism, and mutual support. By encouraging a growth mindset, developing adaptability through skill-building, creating a strong support network, promoting self-care, and reinforcing resilience as a core value, leaders prepare their team to face future transitions with confidence. In this resilient culture, team members feel empowered to embrace change, learn from challenges, and approach each new opportunity as a step toward growth and success.

Becoming A Leader of Influence and inspiration

Leading by Example

Leading by example is one of the most powerful ways to inspire and influence a team. Leaders who model the behaviors, values, and standards they expect from others create an environment where integrity, dedication, and accountability are valued and practiced. When team members see their leader consistently embody the qualities they admire, they feel inspired to adopt those qualities themselves, creating a positive ripple effect throughout the team. Leaders who lead by example build credibility, foster trust, and set a foundation for long-lasting influence.

Leading by example requires consistency, humility, and a commitment to continuous growth. By demonstrating the behaviors and values you want to see in your team, you create a culture where everyone feels empowered to contribute their best, knowing that their leader is right there with them, setting the tone and guiding the way.

Integrity is the cornerstone of effective leadership. Leaders who act with integrity are honest, transparent, and reliable, creating a sense of trust and respect within the team. By consistently acting in alignment with your values, you demonstrate that integrity is more than a concept; it's a guiding principle that shapes decisions, interactions, and outcomes. Integrity inspires loyalty, as team members feel confident in their leader's intentions and decisions.

To lead with integrity, commit to honesty and transparency in all aspects of your work. Follow through on promises, even when it's challenging, and be willing to acknowledge mistakes openly. For example, if a decision doesn't yield the desired outcome, acknowledge it and discuss what can be learned, saying something like, "We took a risk with this approach, and it didn't work as expected. Let's take this as a learning opportunity to adjust our strategy." This openness reinforces your commitment to accountability and honesty, showing team members that integrity includes owning both successes and setbacks.

Accountability is equally essential for leading by example. Leaders who hold themselves accountable set a standard for the team, showing that responsibility is a shared value. Demonstrate accountability by setting high standards for your work, meeting deadlines, and taking ownership of your role's impact on the team. When team members see that you're accountable to the same standards they are, they're more likely to follow suit, creating a culture of responsibility and reliability.

A strong work ethic is an inspiring quality that reflects commitment, discipline, and dedication. Leaders who demonstrate a robust work ethic encourage their team to approach their roles with the same level of enthusiasm and focus. By setting high standards for your own work, you create a culture of excellence where each team member feels motivated to contribute their best.

To embody a strong work ethic, approach your responsibilities with enthusiasm and dedication. Show up consistently, meet deadlines, and strive for quality in everything you do. When challenges arise, demonstrate resilience and perseverance, maintaining a positive attitude even in difficult circumstances. For example, if the team faces a tight deadline, show your commitment by working alongside them, providing support and guidance to help everyone stay motivated.

Encourage your team to adopt the same work ethic by celebrating examples of dedication and focus. Recognize team members who go above and beyond, showing that hard work is valued and appreciated. This focus on excellence creates a positive cycle, where everyone feels inspired to bring their best effort to every task, knowing that their leader is doing the same.

Leaders who commit to continuous learning and self-improvement set an example of adaptability and growth. By embracing a mindset of learning, you show that growth is a lifelong journey and that there's always room for improvement. This commitment to personal development inspires team members to seek out opportunities for growth, as they see that their leader values curiosity, exploration, and knowledge.

Demonstrate a commitment to learning by staying informed about industry trends, pursuing professional development opportunities, and seeking feedback on your performance. For instance, attend relevant workshops or conferences, and share insights with your team, showing that you're actively working to improve your skills. Let your team know that you're open to feedback, and invite them to offer their insights, saying something like, "I'm always looking to improve, so I appreciate any feedback you can provide on how I can support you better."

This openness to learning not only reinforces your commitment to growth but also fosters a culture of continuous improvement within the team. When team members see that you're willing to adapt and grow, they feel encouraged to approach their own roles with curiosity and a commitment to development.

Empathy and compassion are essential qualities for leaders who want to connect meaningfully with their team. Leaders who approach interactions with empathy build trust and rapport, creating an environment where team members feel supported, valued, and understood. By demonstrating genuine care for each person's well-being, you inspire loyalty and commitment, as team members see that their leader is invested in their success.

Show empathy by actively listening to team members, responding to their concerns, and offering support during challenging times. Approach each interaction with patience, making an effort to understand different perspectives and needs. For example, if a team member is struggling with a heavy workload, express empathy by acknowledging their efforts, asking how you can help, and offering solutions that provide relief. This compassionate approach reinforces your commitment to the team's well-being, creating a supportive, positive atmosphere.

Compassionate leadership also involves celebrating personal and professional milestones, recognizing team members as individuals with unique goals and accomplishments. By taking the time to acknowledge these moments, you show that each person's journey is valued, reinforcing a sense of belonging and appreciation.

Leaders who promote collaboration and teamwork set a powerful example, demonstrating that success is a collective effort. By emphasizing the value of collaboration, you create a culture where team members feel inspired to support each other, share knowledge, and work together toward common goals. Leaders who embrace teamwork foster a sense of unity, helping everyone see that they're part of something larger than themselves.

Promote collaboration by actively involving yourself in team activities, whether by participating in group discussions, offering support during collaborative projects, or sharing insights openly. For instance, join brainstorming sessions, contribute ideas, and encourage others to do the same, creating an inclusive environment where everyone feels comfortable sharing their perspectives. This hands-on approach shows that you're committed to the team's success, not just your own.

Celebrate examples of teamwork by recognizing collaborative efforts and expressing appreciation for each team member's contribution. For example, after a successful project, acknowledge how each person's role contributed to the outcome, reinforcing the value of working together. This focus on teamwork builds camaraderie, as team members see that their leader values and celebrates collective success.

Leading by example is a powerful way to inspire and influence your team. By demonstrating integrity, embodying a strong work ethic, embracing continuous learning, cultivating empathy, and promoting collaboration, you create a culture where team members feel motivated to follow your lead and contribute their best. Through your actions, you set the standard for excellence, building a team that's inspired to approach each challenge with dedication, enthusiasm, and a commitment to shared success.

Building Authentic Relationships with Your Team

Authentic relationships are the foundation of effective leadership. Leaders who prioritize connection, honesty, and understanding create a culture where team members feel valued, respected, and motivated to contribute. By taking the time to get to know each team member personally and professionally, leaders build trust and inspire loyalty, making it easier for everyone to collaborate, communicate, and stay committed to shared goals.

Building authentic relationships requires empathy, genuine interest, and a commitment to mutual respect. When team members feel that their leader truly understands and cares for them, they're more likely to trust, open up, and engage with the team's mission. Authentic connections create a positive, supportive work environment where everyone feels empowered to achieve their full potential.

Taking the time to understand each team member as an individual is a powerful way to build authentic relationships. Leaders who make an effort to learn about team members' backgrounds, interests, and aspirations demonstrate respect and appreciation, creating a foundation of trust. By understanding each person's unique strengths, motivations, and goals, you can provide more personalized support, guidance, and encouragement.

During one-on-one meetings or informal conversations, ask open-ended questions that invite team members to share more about themselves. For example, you might ask, "What aspects of your work are most meaningful to you?" or "Are there any personal goals you're working toward outside of work?" Show genuine interest in their responses, listening attentively and acknowledging their experiences.

When leaders know team members' strengths and preferences, they can assign tasks and roles that align with each person's skills and interests. This approach fosters a sense of purpose and engagement, as team members feel that their contributions are valued and that their leader understands their unique qualities.

Active listening is essential for building authentic relationships, as it demonstrates respect, empathy, and a willingness to understand others' perspectives. Leaders who listen attentively to their team create an environment where everyone feels heard and valued, strengthening trust and encouraging open dialogue. Active listening also allows leaders to respond thoughtfully, making team members feel that their insights and concerns are taken seriously.

Practice active listening by focusing fully on the speaker, maintaining eye contact, and avoiding interruptions. Show that you're engaged by nodding, asking clarifying questions, or summarizing key points to confirm understanding. For example, after a team member shares a concern, you might say, "It sounds like you're feeling overwhelmed by the new project timeline. Let's discuss ways we can manage the workload effectively." This response shows that you've listened carefully and are willing to address their needs.

Encourage open communication by creating opportunities for team members to share their ideas, feedback, and concerns. Foster a culture where everyone feels comfortable speaking up, whether during team meetings, one-on-one discussions, or informal chats. By practicing active listening and promoting open dialogue, you build stronger, more trusting relationships that enhance collaboration and engagement.

Expressing appreciation is a powerful way to build authentic relationships, as it reinforces team members' sense of value and motivation. Leaders who consistently recognize each person's contributions create a culture where team members feel seen, respected, and motivated to do their best. Genuine appreciation goes beyond formal recognition; it's about acknowledging the unique strengths and efforts that each person brings to the team.

Show appreciation by recognizing specific contributions, whether it's a job well done on a project, a supportive gesture toward a colleague, or an innovative idea that enhances the team's work. For example, after a team member leads a successful presentation, you might say, "Your attention to detail really showed in that presentation. Thank you for putting in the extra effort—it made a big difference." This specific recognition reinforces their unique strengths, making them feel valued for who they are.

In addition to individual recognition, celebrate team achievements collectively, acknowledging the contributions of each person involved. This inclusive approach reinforces camaraderie and shows that each person's efforts are appreciated as part of the team's success.

Authentic relationships are built on transparency and a willingness to be vulnerable. Leaders who are open about their own experiences, challenges, and growth journey create an environment where team members feel safe to do the same. By demonstrating vulnerability, you show that it's okay to have questions, make mistakes, or seek support, fostering a culture of trust and mutual respect.

To encourage transparency, share your own experiences openly, including both successes and setbacks. For example, if you're implementing a new strategy, admit if there are aspects you're still learning and invite team members to provide feedback or insights. You might say, "I'm still getting comfortable with this new approach, so I appreciate any feedback you have as we work through it together." This openness creates a collaborative environment where team members feel empowered to share their thoughts and ask questions without fear of judgment.

Encourage team members to be transparent by creating a safe space for open communication. Emphasize that honesty is valued and that everyone is encouraged to bring their full selves to work. This culture of vulnerability strengthens relationships, as team members feel understood and supported, knowing that their leader values authenticity.

Leaders who are invested in their team members' growth demonstrate genuine care and commitment, creating deeper, more meaningful connections. When team members see that their leader is dedicated to their development, they feel motivated to contribute their best, knowing that their goals and aspirations are valued. Supporting both personal and professional growth builds loyalty, as team members feel encouraged to pursue their potential within a supportive environment.

During one-on-one discussions, ask team members about their goals, strengths, and areas where they'd like to grow. Collaborate on creating a development plan that includes both skill-building and opportunities for personal growth, such as leadership training, public speaking, or time management. For example, if a team member expresses interest in improving their presentation skills, suggest workshops or offer to provide feedback after practice sessions. This guidance shows that you're genuinely invested in their growth journey.

Encourage team members to pursue personal development goals outside of work, showing that you value their well-being and personal growth. For instance, if someone is training for a marathon or learning a new language, express support and celebrate milestones along the way. By supporting their growth holistically, you reinforce your commitment to each team member as a whole person, not just as an employee.

Building authentic relationships with your team fosters a culture of trust, respect, and collaboration. By getting to know each team member personally and professionally, practicing active listening, showing appreciation, encouraging transparency, and supporting growth, leaders create a positive environment where everyone feels valued and engaged. These genuine connections empower team members to contribute their best, approach challenges with confidence, and stay motivated to achieve shared goals.

Empowering Your Team to Lead and Grow

Empowering team members to lead and grow is essential for building a high-performing, resilient, and motivated team. Leaders who provide opportunities for autonomy, decision-making, and skill development help their team members develop confidence, take ownership of their work, and build their capabilities. Empowering others creates a positive cycle, where each person feels encouraged to pursue their potential and actively contribute to the team's success. By fostering empowerment, you create a culture where everyone feels motivated to lead, learn, and grow.

Empowerment requires trust, delegation, and a commitment to each team member's development. When leaders empower their team, they cultivate a collaborative, growth-oriented environment where everyone feels confident in their abilities and inspired to contribute.

Delegation is a powerful way to empower team members, as it gives them the opportunity to take on new challenges, make decisions, and develop their skills. Leaders who delegate responsibility and authority show that they trust their team, encouraging team members to take ownership and approach their roles with confidence. By delegating effectively, you foster a culture where each person feels valued and capable, motivated to rise to new levels of responsibility.

When delegating tasks, consider each team member's strengths, skills, and areas for growth. Assign tasks that challenge them while aligning with their abilities and interests. For example, if a team member has shown skill in strategic thinking, delegate a portion of project planning to them, providing guidance as needed but allowing them to take the lead. This approach gives them the chance to develop further while contributing meaningfully to the team's objectives.

Empower team members by giving them the authority to

make decisions within their areas of responsibility. Communicate clear expectations and outcomes but allow them the freedom to determine the best approach. This autonomy reinforces trust, as team members see that their leader respects their judgment and abilities, motivating them to take ownership of their roles.

Empowerment flourishes in an environment where initiative and innovation are encouraged. Leaders who inspire their team to think creatively and explore new ideas foster a culture of continuous improvement, where everyone feels empowered to contribute fresh perspectives. By promoting initiative, you help team members see that their ideas are valued and that they have the power to drive positive change.

Encourage initiative by creating a safe space for experimentation and new ideas. Invite team members to share their thoughts, suggestions, and potential solutions for current projects or challenges. For example, you might say, "If you have any ideas on how we can improve our process, please share. I'd love to hear your perspective." This openness creates a culture where innovation is celebrated, and team members feel empowered to think beyond conventional approaches.

Support team members who take initiative by providing guidance and recognizing their efforts, even if the outcome doesn't go as planned. Reinforce the value of learning from experience, emphasizing that every attempt contributes to growth. By celebrating initiative, you create a culture where everyone feels encouraged to take risks and explore new possibilities.

Empowering your team includes providing opportunities for skill development and leadership growth. Leaders who support professional development create a pathway for team members to reach their potential, whether by enhancing current skills or preparing for future roles. By investing in their growth, you show that you're committed to their success and believe in their capacity to lead and contribute.

Offer a range of development opportunities, from workshops and online courses to mentorship programs and hands-on leadership experiences. For example, if a team member is interested in project management, assign them a lead role in an upcoming project, providing mentorship and feedback along the way. This hands-on experience builds confidence, reinforcing their ability to lead and make decisions effectively.

Encourage team members to set personal development goals and explore areas they'd like to strengthen. Check in regularly to discuss their progress, provide support, and celebrate achievements. By supporting each person's growth, you empower them to take ownership of their development, helping them build the skills and confidence needed to step into leadership roles.

Accountability is a key component of empowerment, as it encourages team members to take responsibility for their roles and actions. Leaders who foster a culture of accountability create an environment where everyone feels motivated to meet their commitments, contribute meaningfully, and support the team's success. By emphasizing ownership, you help team members see the importance of their contributions, empowering them to take pride in their work.

Promote accountability by setting clear expectations, providing constructive feedback, and encouraging team members to take ownership of their goals. For instance, if a team member is responsible for a specific task, discuss the outcomes you expect, and let them know that they have full ownership of the project. Check in regularly to offer guidance and celebrate progress, showing that you're there to support them while respecting their autonomy.

Encourage team members to hold themselves accountable by setting their own goals and tracking their progress. This self-directed approach reinforces a sense of responsibility and empowerment, as team members feel invested in their success and motivated to achieve their objectives. By promoting accountability, you create a culture where each person takes ownership of their work, strengthening their confidence and commitment.

Recognition is an essential part of empowerment, as it reinforces each person's progress and contributions. Leaders who celebrate growth and achievement create a positive, motivating environment where team members feel valued and inspired to continue developing. By recognizing individual and team successes, you encourage a culture of celebration, where everyone feels encouraged to pursue their potential and take on new challenges.

Acknowledge individual achievements by celebrating both small and large milestones. For example, if a team member successfully leads their first project, recognize their effort and growth, saying something like, "Your leadership on this project made a real difference. Thank you for taking on this challenge and making it a success." This specific recognition reinforces their confidence, showing that their growth is valued and appreciated.

Celebrate team achievements by highlighting collaborative efforts, showing that each person's contribution played a role in the success. Express gratitude for the team's hard work, resilience, and innovation, emphasizing the value of working together. This recognition not only boosts morale but also reinforces a culture of support, where everyone feels inspired to take ownership and contribute to the team's success.

Empowering your team to lead and grow builds a culture of autonomy, responsibility, and continuous improvement. By delegating responsibility, encouraging initiative, providing development opportunities, promoting accountability, and celebrating achievements, leaders create an environment where everyone feels motivated to pursue their potential and contribute meaningfully. This culture of empowerment inspires team members to embrace leadership, approach challenges with confidence, and drive the team toward shared success.

Inspiring a Vision and Purpose for the Future

A clear and inspiring vision gives a team a sense of purpose, direction, and motivation. Leaders who articulate a compelling vision help their team see beyond day-to-day tasks, connecting their work to meaningful goals that extend beyond the present. When team members understand how their contributions support a larger purpose, they feel inspired, engaged, and committed, ready to navigate challenges and contribute to shared success. By inspiring with vision, you foster a culture of optimism and purpose, where everyone feels motivated to work toward a brighter future.

Creating an inspiring vision requires clarity, passion, and a commitment to aligning team goals with the organization's mission. When leaders communicate this vision effectively, they empower team members to see the impact of their work, making it easier for everyone to stay focused, motivated, and dedicated to the team's long-term success.

An effective vision is clear, ambitious, and aligned with both the team's values and the organization's mission. Leaders who take the time to define a meaningful vision provide their team with a sense of direction and purpose, making it easier for everyone to stay motivated and committed to shared goals. By creating a vision that resonates, you inspire your team to work together toward a common objective.

To define your vision, start by identifying the core values, goals, and outcomes that are most meaningful to the team and the organization. Consider both short-term objectives and long-term aspirations, asking questions like, "What impact do we want to make?" or "How do we want to grow together?" This reflection helps you craft a vision that aligns with your team's strengths, values, and goals.

Once you've defined the vision, articulate it in a way that's both clear and inspiring. Use concise, impactful language that captures the essence of your purpose. For example, if your vision is to become a leader in customer satisfaction, you might say, "Our goal is to set the standard for exceptional customer service, building lasting relationships and exceeding expectations at every turn." This clarity reinforces your team's purpose, giving everyone a shared goal to work toward.

A compelling vision must be communicated with passion and consistency to resonate with the team. Leaders who share their vision enthusiastically and frequently create an environment where team members feel excited about the future, inspired to contribute, and connected to a larger purpose. By communicating the vision regularly, you reinforce its importance, ensuring that it remains a guiding force in the team's work.

Share your vision during team meetings, project updates, and one-on-one discussions, emphasizing how each person's contributions align with the larger goals. Use stories, examples, or anecdotes that illustrate the vision in action, helping team members see the impact of their work. For instance, if your vision involves innovating new solutions, share examples of recent projects where team creativity led to positive results. This storytelling approach makes the vision tangible, inspiring team members to see their role in bringing it to life.

Be consistent in your messaging, reinforcing the vision at every opportunity. Connect daily tasks and objectives to the broader vision, showing team members how their efforts contribute to long-term goals. This regular reinforcement keeps the vision at the forefront, reminding everyone of the purpose that drives their work.

Aligning team goals with the vision ensures that everyone is working in the same direction, motivated by shared purpose. Leaders who connect individual objectives to the broader vision create a sense of unity, where each team member sees how their work contributes to collective success. By aligning goals, you create a pathway that makes the vision achievable, encouraging team members to stay focused and motivated.

When setting team goals, ensure they reflect the values, priorities, and outcomes described in the vision. For instance, if your vision emphasizes innovation, set goals that encourage creative problem-solving, new project ideas, or product development. Clearly communicate how each goal supports the vision, making it easier for team members to see the purpose behind their tasks.

Encourage team members to set individual goals that align with the vision, fostering a sense of personal ownership and motivation. Discuss how each person's unique strengths contribute to achieving the vision, reinforcing that everyone has a vital role to play. This alignment helps team members feel invested in the shared purpose, making it easier for them to approach their roles with dedication and enthusiasm.

Involving the team in shaping the vision creates a sense of ownership, where each member feels personally connected to the goals and outcomes. Leaders who invite team members to contribute ideas, share perspectives, and provide input make the vision a collaborative effort, fostering a culture of inclusivity and commitment. When team members have a hand in defining the vision, they feel more motivated to work toward it, as they see it as a shared goal that reflects their values and aspirations.

Create opportunities for team members to contribute to the vision, whether through brainstorming sessions, feedback forums, or one-on-one discussions. Invite them to share their ideas, insights, and hopes for the future, showing that their perspectives are valued. For example, you might ask, "What do you see as our team's biggest opportunity for growth?" or "How do you envision our impact in the next few years?" This inclusive approach empowers team members to co-create the vision, strengthening their commitment to achieving it.

As the vision evolves, continue to involve the team in discussions and updates, ensuring that everyone feels included and informed. This collaboration reinforces a culture of shared ownership, where each person feels invested in the vision and motivated to bring it to life.

Celebrating achievements that align with the vision reinforces its importance, making it clear that each step forward contributes to long-term success. Leaders who recognize and celebrate progress create a positive, motivating environment where team members feel appreciated for their contributions. By linking recognition to the vision, you inspire team members to stay engaged, knowing that their efforts are valued and impactful.

Acknowledge individual and team achievements that move the team closer to the vision. For example, if your vision emphasizes customer satisfaction, celebrate team members who go above and beyond to support clients, recognizing their dedication to the shared goal. Express appreciation for their efforts, saying something like, "Your commitment to helping our clients is a powerful example of our vision in action. Thank you for bringing us closer to our goal of exceptional service."

Additionally, celebrate milestones in the journey toward the vision, whether it's completing a major project, reaching a performance benchmark, or overcoming a challenge. Recognize how each achievement supports the vision, reinforcing the team's motivation to continue working toward it. These celebrations create a sense of progress, reminding everyone that their efforts are contributing to a meaningful purpose.

Inspiring a vision and purpose for the future provides your team with direction, motivation, and a shared sense of purpose. By defining a clear vision, communicating it with passion, aligning goals, involving the team, and reinforcing progress through recognition, leaders create an environment where everyone feels motivated to contribute. This culture of purpose and optimism empowers each team member to work toward a brighter future, confident in the knowledge that their efforts support a meaningful, shared goal.

Leaving a Legacy of Leadership

A legacy of leadership is the impact a leader leaves behind, shaping the culture, values, and vision of the team long after their tenure ends. Leaders who focus on their legacy aim to create a lasting, positive influence that extends beyond their direct presence. By building strong relationships, fostering growth, and inspiring commitment to a shared purpose, these leaders empower their team to continue growing, innovating, and achieving success. A legacy is not about personal accolades; it's about creating a foundation of values and practices that empower others to lead and excel.

Leaving a legacy of leadership requires intention, consistency, and a dedication to building something meaningful and enduring. When leaders focus on their legacy, they cultivate an environment where team members feel inspired to carry forward the vision, principles, and goals that drive their collective success.

A key aspect of leaving a legacy is cultivating future leaders who can carry forward the team's vision, values, and purpose. Leaders who prioritize development ensure that the team will continue to thrive, innovate, and adapt, even in their absence. By mentoring, guiding, and empowering team members to step into leadership roles, you create a lasting impact that strengthens the team's resilience and potential.

Identify individuals with leadership potential and provide them with opportunities to develop their skills, whether through mentorship, training, or hands-on experience. For instance, if a team member has shown initiative, assign them a leadership role in a project, offering support and feedback along the way. This experience builds their confidence, preparing them to take on more significant responsibilities in the future.

Encourage team members to develop their leadership style, strengths, and goals. By fostering a culture of growth, you create an environment where everyone feels empowered to pursue their potential, ensuring that the team remains strong, adaptable, and driven by shared values, even after you've moved on.

Values and principles are the foundation of any lasting legacy. Leaders who focus on instilling core values—such as integrity, collaboration, and accountability—create a culture where team members feel aligned, motivated, and inspired to work toward common goals. By emphasizing these values, you ensure that they remain integral to the team's identity, guiding decisions, actions, and relationships long into the future.

Define the values that matter most to you and the team, using them as guiding principles in all decisions, interactions, and practices. For example, if integrity is a core value, model honesty and transparency, even when it's challenging. This consistency reinforces the importance of values, showing team members that they're more than words—they're a shared commitment to doing what's right.

Reinforce these values regularly, whether through team discussions, recognition of value-driven actions, or sharing stories that highlight their importance. By making values a central part of the team's culture, you create a legacy where future team members feel empowered to carry these principles forward, ensuring that they remain part of the team's foundation.

Legacy is often reinforced by the systems and processes that support a team's goals, culture, and effectiveness. Leaders who build efficient, adaptable processes create a structure that helps the team thrive long after they're gone. These systems provide continuity, making it easier for future leaders to maintain quality, achieve objectives, and navigate challenges with confidence.

Identify key areas where systems or processes could support long-term success, such as communication, project management, or performance evaluation. Create frameworks that simplify tasks, enhance collaboration, or streamline workflows, ensuring that they're clear, effective, and adaptable. For instance, develop a process for project planning that includes templates, best practices, and checklists, making it easier for team members to manage projects consistently.

Document these processes and provide training, making sure that team members are familiar with how they work and why they're beneficial. By establishing reliable, efficient systems, you create a foundation that supports the team's resilience, helping them sustain high performance and continuity through future transitions.

Leaders who leave a legacy celebrate the collective achievements of their team, reinforcing a culture of gratitude, recognition, and pride. By highlighting the team's contributions, you show that the legacy is not yours alone—it's a shared accomplishment shaped by everyone's efforts and dedication. This celebration of collective success fosters a sense of ownership, where each person feels motivated to continue building on the team's achievements.

Acknowledge individual and team milestones regularly, expressing appreciation for each contribution. Recognize both large accomplishments, like completing major projects, and small wins, such as personal growth or overcoming challenges. For example, if the team successfully reaches a performance target, celebrate their hard work, saying something like, "Your commitment has brought us to this achievement. This success belongs to all of you."

Encourage team members to celebrate each other's accomplishments, creating a culture where everyone's contributions are valued and appreciated. This positive atmosphere inspires each person to take pride in their work, ensuring that the team's legacy of excellence, gratitude, and support endures.

A lasting legacy is one that encourages continuous improvement, where each generation of team members is motivated to innovate, adapt, and strive for excellence. Leaders who foster a growth mindset create a culture of resilience and progress, inspiring team members to build on existing successes while seeking new opportunities for growth.

Encourage a culture of learning, where team members feel empowered to pursue new skills, explore innovative ideas, and seek constructive feedback. For example, provide opportunities for skill development, host knowledge-sharing sessions, or establish regular feedback loops. This commitment to improvement reinforces the idea that growth is an ongoing journey, not a final destination.

Celebrate examples of continuous improvement, whether it's a team member who develops a new skill, a process that enhances productivity, or a successful project that reflects the team's dedication to excellence. By making growth a core value, you create a legacy where each person feels inspired to pursue their potential, ensuring that the team remains adaptable and progressive in the years to come.

Leaving a legacy of leadership is about creating a positive, lasting impact that empowers your team to thrive long into the future. By cultivating future leaders, instilling core values, establishing lasting systems, celebrating achievements, and inspiring continuous improvement, you build a foundation of excellence, resilience, and purpose. This legacy of leadership not only supports your team's success but also ensures that the values, vision, and principles you've championed continue to guide and inspire the team, making a lasting difference for years to come.

ABOUT THE AUTHOR

Jerry Brittain is a seasoned leader, lifelong learner, and passionate advocate for empowering individuals to reach their full potential. With extensive experience in people development, operations management, and team building, Jerry has spent his career helping organizations and individuals thrive by fostering cultures of collaboration, growth, and purpose.

Currently pursuing a Doctorate in Business Administration, Jerry combines academic insight with practical leadership experience to deliver actionable strategies that inspire others to lead with integrity and impact. His professional journey includes leading high-performing teams, navigating complex organizational challenges, and driving continuous improvement in diverse settings. Jerry's dedication to leadership development extends beyond the workplace, as he actively mentors aspiring leaders and shares his expertise through workshops and coaching.

When he's not writing, Jerry enjoys spending time outdoors and exploring creative outlets such as storytelling. His commitment to personal and professional growth serves as a testament to the principles he shares in this book, offering readers a roadmap for leading with purpose and leaving a lasting legacy.